POST-WAR YORKSHIRE AIRFIELDS

Spitfire LF.16e TB308 (officially 7255M from March 1958) at RAF Norton, Sheffield, about 1960. The large sheds in the background were the barrage balloon sheds built during the Second World War to help with the defence of Sheffield. (ADT)

Spitfire Vb BM597 mounted guard at Church Fenton from 1957 until 1989 except for a short period at Linton-on-Ouse in the late 1970s. It had the distinction of being used to create the master moulds for the Spitfire 'scenery' replicas in the film, *Battle of Britain*. It is painted as 'PR-O' to commemorate No.609 (West Riding of Yorkshire) Squadron Auxiliary Air Force which flew the type early in the Second World War. Reformed in the Royal Auxiliary Air Force originally at Yeadon, No.609 (West Riding) Squadron was based at Church Fenton flying Gloster Meteors until disbandment in 1957.

The policy to sell-off certain gate guard airframes suffering from the elements resulted in BM597 being civilian-registered as G-MKVB in 1989. It was fully restored to flying condition at Duxford, Cambridgeshire, as 'JH-C', markings it wore during the Second World War when flying with No.317 (Polish) Squadron RAF.

POST-WAR YORKSHIRE AIRFIELDS

Barry Abraham

TEMPUS

No.202 Squadron was based at Finningley – their badge is shown on the sliding fuselage door of this Westland Whirlwind HAR.10 XJ724. The aircraft was displayed at Leeming on 14 June 1970 a Royal Observer Corps day, following the Vale of York air display.

First published 2002
Copyright © Barry Abraham, 2002

Tempus Publishing Limited
The Mill, Brimscombe Port,
Stroud, Gloucestershire, GL5 2QG

ISBN 0 7524 2390 8

Typesetting and origination by
Tempus Publishing Limited
Printed in Great Britain by
Midway Colour Print, Wiltshire

Contents

Acknowledgements

In the search for relevant photographs, I am especially indebted to Frank Cheesman; Harry Holmes; Steve Gillard (Brough Heritage Centre); Derrick Milner; Peter Naylor (Memorial Room RAF Linton-on-Ouse); Norman Smart and Ray Sturtivant. Also, Ashley Bailey; Phil Butler; Bob Davies; Iain Dick; Dick Dodwell; Aldon Ferguson; Dennis Flather; Barry Jones, *Aeroplane Monthly*; John Kendrick; Martin Locke (CRO RAF Shawbury); Leo Marriot; Barry Morse; Gerald Myers; Derek Nimmo; Lloyd Robinson/Brian Robinson Collection; Rodney Robinson; Michael J.Rutter, *Slingsby Aviation*; Jim Stuart; David E. Thompson; Alex D. Turner; Mrs Gill Yeoman and *The Yorkshire Post*. Geoff Simmons managed to make good prints from my negatives of aircraft at other airfields and provided some of the Driffield prints. I am grateful for their assistance.

Most of the photographs have been taken by the author, but unfortunately a number donated over the years have not identified the photographer. Where possible, I have tried to establish the name of the photographer, but in some cases it has eluded me so I am sorry if credit has not been given.

A number of books have been consulted to check information:
Avro: The History of an Aircraft Company by Harry Holmes; *Mother Worked at Avro* by Gerald Myers; *British Independent Airlines Since 1946* (original editions); *Blackburn Aircraft Since 1909* by A.J. Jackson; *British Civil Aircraft Since 1919* Vols I-III by A.J. Jackson; *Clifton, York – The Airport That Never Was* by Norman Spence, Guy Jefferson and Ian Robinson; *Control Towers* by Paul Francis; *Aviation in Doncaster* by Geoffrey Oakes; *Flying at Sherburn* by John Facer; *RAF Serials* by J.J. Halley; *The Squadrons of the RAF & Commonwealth* by J.J. Halley and *RAF Training & Support Units* by Ray Sturtivant et al, both published by Air-Britain; and the invaluable *Wrecks & Relics* by Ken Ellis.

Magazines include *Airfield Review*, the journal of the Airfield Research Group, and members of the Group who have provided advice and information.

My wife Penelope for her patience and navigating me around the Yorkshire airfields over the last thirty-five years or so.

An interesting visitor to Sherburn on 8 September 2001 was this privately owned North American P-51 Mustang, parked on the grass in front of the wartime Air Transport Auxiliary hangar.

Introduction

At the end of the Second World War, Yorkshire had a considerable number of airfields ranging from the few pre-war civil aerodromes, the 1930s RAF expansion airfields and many temporary airfields built for the duration. Most of the war period airfields were constructed to accommodate bomber squadrons supported by a few fighter stations in defence of the industrial areas. The large numbers of servicemen and service women had left and civilian companies were beginning to get back into the business. Many of the airfields were closed and the permanent stations were designated for flying training purposes, others used as Reserve Landing Grounds or for the storage and disposal of surplus equipment including explosives by the RAF.

Agriculture took over at the deserted airfields, very necessary in post-war Britain, but in the 1950s, with the heightening of the cold war situation, some of the airfields were rebuilt, fighter squadrons came and the advent of the 'V' bomber and missile forces resulted in Yorkshire becoming a key military area once again. The next decade brought wholesale selling off surplus land which had been used for the airfields and buildings were allowed to become derelict or were demolished, hangars survived for storage and derelict taxiways or runways used for motor racing etc. In recent years, former serving personnel have raised by their own subscription money to have a memorial placed at their old airfields, to remember their comrades, many of whom did not return.

A major military aviation presence is currently maintained in the Vale of York, with Leeming, Dishforth, Topcliffe, Linton-on-Ouse and Church Fenton in regular use. Despite the reduced size of the RAF, Yorkshire remains an important area with Tornado squadrons and extensive flying training in the area.

The open areas of the former airfields were attractive to private flying and wartime concrete adapted, thriving clubs catering for both powered and glider aircraft were formed. Civilian flying now proliferates especially at Sherburn-in-Elmet and Breighton as well as at Leeds-Bradford with gliding sites at Sutton Bank, Burn, Rufforth and Pocklington. One of the finest aviation museums in Britain has been opened at the former wartime airfield at Elvington, near York.

The municipal airport of Leeds-Bradford has been developed as a major international airport and a brand new airport opened at Sheffield. The former RAF station at Middleton St. George became Teesside Airport and moved out of Yorkshire under local government re-organisation. Plans exist to develop the onetime RAF 'V' bomber base at Finningley as a civil airport.

To cover every airfield in Yorkshire adequately would need a very large book. Some airfields have had to be omitted, mainly because there is little to see. In a similar way, some RAF units and civil flying clubs are not mentioned because of lack of space or suitable illustrations found. The same-type aircraft operated at different airfields have not been duplicated to try to give space to other types.

Apologies if anything has been left out!

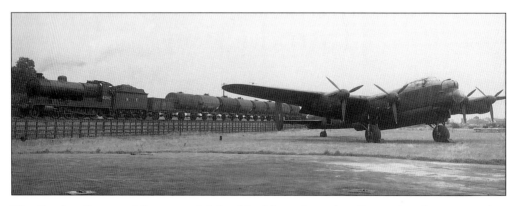

The Bomber Command Instructors' School had been formed at Finningley during 1944 but moved to Scampton in Lincolnshire at the beginning of 1947. This Lancaster DV200 is parked on the dispersals on the north side of the airfield next to the North Eastern Railway line. It had seen operations over enemy territory but relegated to training and eventually Struck Off Charge in 1946 after the war had ended. (BM)

The former First World War aerodrome at Tadcaster, known initially as Bramham Moor, has all but disappeared under agriculture. However, the wooden bow-strung truss hangar, photographed in 1972, continues to survive and clearly seen from the A64 road.

Typical of the light aircraft used in the 1950s is this Percival Proctor III G-AKWV at Sherburn-in-Elmet on 6 August 1951. During the war it had been used for radio training, communications with the American forces and civilianised in 1948. (HH)

One

Military Airfields: Leeming, Catterick & Middleton St George

RAF Leeming

Yorkshire Air Services had used a small landing ground at Leeming and this probably brought Air Ministry attention to the suitability of the area. An adjacent site was selected in 1938 for development as an aerodrome under expansion scheme M, construction commencing in 1939. Leeming was a grass aerodrome with five large Type 'C' hangars of the later version (a lower roof height and sheet cladding on the steel frame). Opened on 3 June 1940 in Bomber Command, Leeming served in No.4 (Bomber) Group and then No.6 (RCAF) Group, which controlled the Canadian squadrons in North Yorkshire. Leeming was scheduled for retention and passed to Fighter Command as the home of No.54 Operational Training Unit in 1946. It became No.228 (Tactical Light Bomber & Night Fighter) Operational Conversion Unit in 1947 and used a variety of aircraft such as Mosquito T.3, FB.6, NF.30, NF.36; Wellington T.18; Oxford T.1; Martinet TT.1; Brigand B.1,T.4; Valetta C.1, T.3, T.4; Javelin FAW.5, FAW.7; Canberra T.4, T.11 until it was disbanded in 1961. During this time, No.33 Squadron flying Meteor NF.14 and Javelin FAW.7 aircraft was based at Leeming. The airfield and runways at Leeming have been constantly improved over the years and in 1956 the station was rebuilt.

In 1961 Leeming was transferred to Flying Training Command and No.3 Flying Training School was reformed, flying Jet Provost, Chipmunk, Vampire and Bulldog aircraft. Dishforth was also used as a Reserve Landing Ground until the school was disbanded in 1984. The Northumbrian UAS and No.11 Air Experience Flight with Chipmunk T.10 and Bulldog T.1 were based there until Leeming was once again closed for rebuilding, including Hardened Aircraft Shelters and a new Air Traffic Control in 1985. When reopened in 1988, Leeming was transferred to Strike Command with No.11 Squadron and No.23 Squadron being reformed and equipped with the Tornado F.3 to be joined by No.25 Squadron. Northumbrian UAS/11 AEF also returned.

Catterick

The history of flying at Catterick goes back to 1915 when the first training squadrons were formed within the Royal Flying Corps. A large number of these small units served at Catterick until the end of the First World War. In the late 1920s the RAF reformed No.26 (Army Co-operation) Squadron at Catterick to work with local army units and they remained right up to the beginning of the Second World War. During the late 1930s, the station buildings and airfield were updated with the construction of new Type 'C' hangars and a control tower. Fighter Command rotated squadrons for rest periods to Catterick during the Battle of Britain and later various squadrons for local defence and 'working up' prior to operations elsewhere.

After the Second World War, the airfield had remained grass surfaced, the buildings were used for storage of equipment and in 1959 the RAF Fire & Rescue Training Unit came from Sutton-on-Hull, taking on a number of obsolete aircraft for this necessary training until disbandment in 1988. Catterick was also the RAF Regiment Depot until 1994 and then it became the British Army Marne Barracks.

Middleton St George

Like Leeming, this site was planned as an expansion scheme M aerodrome with construction starting in 1939 but opening was delayed until 1941, with the result that the hangars were of a mixed variety. Taken over in 1941 by No.4 Group Bomber Command for No.78 (Bomber) Squadron flying Whitleys (later returning with Handley Page Halifaxes) and No.76 (Bomber) with Halifaxes, the airfield was passed over the Canadian bomber squadrons in No.6 Group. After the war there was a short period under Fighter Command controlling No.13 OTU which merged with No.54 OTU to form No.228 OCU at Leeming. Middleton St George was passed to Flying Training Command initially for use as an Air Navigation School and then a Meteor-equipped Advanced Flying Training School. Expansion of Fighter Command brought a runway extension and strengthening and the arrival of fighter squadrons, flying Hunters and Meteor night fighters, later replaced by Javelins, and then the arrival of the new interceptor, the Lightning and No.226 OCU was formed. It was announced in 1964 that the RAF was to vacate Middleton St George and the airport was purchased by the Teesside Airport Committee (North Riding CC, Darlington CBC, Teesside CBC, Hartlepool BC, Guisborough UDC and Saltburn & Marske UDC).

The station buildings, hangars and accommodation with part of the airfield were located in Co. Durham but a large proportion of the airfield and additional areas taken over for expansion were in the North Riding of Yorkshire. Later county boundary changes have somewhat changed this situation.

Leeming fell quiet after the Canadian squadrons left in August 1945 until summer 1946 when taken over by No.54 Operational Training Unit, which had moved in from East Moor airfield situated close to York. The control tower and Signals Square front the Type 'C' hangars, with the well laid out station buildings behind. This view looks almost due south to the Vale of York. (EFC)

The original control tower at Leeming was built in concrete to a standard 1939 design; during hot weather the windows could be rolled back. Access to the balcony was from a side door. On duty, left to right: RTO A.C.W. Saltonstall logging all R/T transmissions, Flt Lt O'Brien, Sgt -?-, Flg Off Burrell, Cpl McCowie. The Mosquito was operated by No.54 OTU in conjunction with training night fighter crews, summer 1946. (EFC)

No.54 OTU was divided up into squadrons with different tasks. No.3 Squadron (AI Training and Drogue Towing) was equipped with Martinets and also Wellingtons. Martinet TT.I NR634 'ST-6' can be identified in the spacious 'C' Type hangar which had, at one time, housed Bomber Command Whitleys, Wellingtons and Halifaxes, October 1946. (EFC)

Staff of No.3 Squadron (AI Training and Drogue towing) No.54 OTU in front of Martinet, October 1946. Left to right: Messrs Glasgow; 'Duke' Lane; Hageman; 'Ginger' Hocking and Hodson. (EFC)

Mosquito NF.XXX outside Hangar No.2, the Leeming hangars being erected later than other expansion period airfields in Yorkshire were of the 'austerity' type without brick or concrete cladding but nevertheless were known as 'protected'. The control tower and fire tender shed are to the rear. (EFC)

Radar Operator Training was carried out by No.3 Squadron of No.54 OTU, Wellington XVIII ND112 was converted for the purpose. The radio operator and navigator's compartment were redesigned to accommodate four pupils, instructor and radar equipment for Airborne Interception training. The front turret was removed from the Wellington with a Mosquito type nose and radar scanner installed. (EFC)

Avro Anson C.19 TX184 was used by 228 OCU as a communications aircraft and appropriately titled 'RAF Leeming'. It is seen here in the company with other aircraft, including what appears to be a French Navy aircraft. The OCU disbanded at Leeming in 1961. (BHA Collection)

No.228 Operational Conversion Unit had the role of Tactical Light Bomber added when it succeeded No.54 OTU and Bristol Brigands such as RH805 coded 'H' were taken on charge at Leeming. Afterwards the OCU equipment changed to Meteor Night Fighters and finally Javelin All Weather Fighters. (BHA Collection)

Acting Pilot Officer Martin Locke, a member of No.3 (Jet Provost) Course at RAF Leeming in 1962. He did 120 hours on the Jet Provost after which he was posted to No.162 Course at Swinderby, Lincolnshire, on the Vampire T 11. (ML)

No.3 FTS, which had reformed at Leeming in 1961, operated the Hunting (later BAC) Jet Provost, including XP663 '35' displayed at the Finningley Battle of Britain Air Display on 18 September 1965. The aircraft were doped silver and carried day-glow orange strips to denote a training aircraft and for better visibility to other aircraft. A variety of patterns were used until a basic half red and half white scheme adopted.

By 1966 the Leeming FTS was known as No.3 (Basic) FTS and used the Jet Provost T.4, such as XP676 '64', 14 June 1970.

The Vintage Pair, popular at many air displays until the unfortunate accident at Coventry, were based at Leeming. They comprised the de Havilland Vampire T.11 XH304 and Gloster Meteor T.7 WF778, both wearing the Central Flying School emblem and authentic Training Command colour scheme of silver aircraft with yellow 'training' bands of 1950s vintage. They are seen here at Finningley on 17 September 1983.

After receiving their 'wings' on the Jet Provost at Leeming, pilots went to RAF Valley in Anglesey, North Wales, for advanced training, initially on the Folland (Hawker Siddeley) Gnat two-seat trainer. No.4 (Advanced) FTS at Valley provided this Gnat XP516 '16' for the Vale of York air display at Leeming, seen above on 14 June 1970. The Gnat was also used by the world famous Red Arrows aerobatic team until replaced by the Hawk.

The Scottish Aviation Bulldog equipped many University Air Squadrons and Air Experience Flights, including those at Leeming. XX619 is on the apron outside Hangar 4 on 10 October 1999. External appearance of this hangar has not changed much but it seems now to be used for other purposes. (DET)

Leeming is now a major Tornado base, having been completely rebuilt, and aircraft are usually kept in the NATO Hardened Aircraft Shelters. This Tornado is from the British element of the Tri-National Tornado Training Establishment based at Cottesmore, with a good view of a Type 'C' hangar dating back to 1939. Photographed 8 November 1995. (LM)

When RAF Finningley closed down, No.100 Squadron relocated to Leeming, sharing the base with the operational Tornado squadrons. Photographed 8 November 1995. (LM)

Catterick was rebuilt earlier than the other expansion period stations in Yorkshire and was provided with a brick watch office with tower (Air Ministry drawing 1959/34). Disused for aviation purposes, the compass bearings remain on the tower (which had a tortuous spiral ladder to climb) but is under threat of demolition. Of about sixteen built in the UK, it is probably the only one remaining of the few built in Yorkshire – others were built of concrete. (BD/DET)

Catterick has not been a flying station since the end of the Second World War with the exception of regular use of the grass airfield by gliders, particularly No.645 (Volunteer) Gliding School. However, some very interesting redundant aircraft found their way to the Fire & Rescue Training Unit. This English Electric Canberra T.4 WJ881 was struck of charge as regards flying on 23 November 1971 and brought (by road) to the RAF Catterick Fire School, as it was noted in April 1973. The shorter version of the substantial brick-clad Type 'C' hangars built in the expansion era and the watch office with tower can also be discerned. (NS)

The control tower at Middleton St George was built in brick (Air Ministry drawing 5845/39) and was subsequently modified by mounting the 1955 design of a Visual Control Room, part of airfield development for fighter operations. Photographed at the time of Teesside Airport, 14 August 1986, but it is substantially same as the RAF period.

No.33 (F) Squadron came to Middleton St George from Leeming on 30 September 1958 with the Gloster Javelin F(AW). 7, later replaced with the F(AW).9. It was disbanded on 17 November 1962. Javelin F(AW). 9 XH911 'J' is on the apron outside the Type 'J' hangar (No.2) at the Battle of Britain display, 16 September 1961. (HH)

Line-up of No.33 (F) Squadron Javelin F(AW). 9 on the apron ready to move out. (DBF)

Javelins of No.33 (F) Squadron taxiing out. (DBF)

Two
Military Airfields: Dishforth & Topcliffe

RAF Dishforth

Opened in 1936 for No.4 (B) Group Bomber Command, RAF Dishforth was one of the earlier expansion scheme bomber stations with a grass flying surface and five substantial Type 'C' hangars. No.10 (Bomber) Squadron with the Handley Page Heyford, later replaced by the Armstrong Whitworth Whitley, was based there and joined by No.78 (Bomber) Squadron, also equipped with the Whitley. Hard runways were built and, still in the role of housing bomber squadrons, Dishforth was handed over to the RCAF in 1942. After the war, Transport Command took over and the first squadron (No.47) to convert to the Handley Page Hastings was based at Dishforth until moving to Topcliffe. The resident training unit became No.241 OCU using Hastings and Avro Yorks and, following a reorganisation, was merged into No.242 OCU in 1951, remaining at Dishforth for more than ten years flying the Valetta, Hastings and Beverley. RLGs were located at Rufforth and nearby Topcliffe aerodromes. During this time No.30 Squadron, also equipped with the Valetta and then the Beverley, was based at Dishforth for about five years.

No.3 FTS at Leeming needed a RLG for training and Dishforth served in this role until 1984. The airfield area held in reserve for Barkston Heath airfield in Lincolnshire, is now being adapted for the Army Air Corps to accommodate their latest helicopters.

RAF Topcliffe

Work commenced in 1939 on another aerodrome for No.4 (B) Group Bomber Command and it opened in 1940 with the arrival of No.77 (Bomber) and 102 (Bomber) Squadrons, flying the Whitley. The station was passed to the Canadians in 1942. Large Type 'C' hangars of the later version with sheet cladding on the steel frame, instead of brick or concrete, were erected. After the war it was allocated to RAF Flying Training Command and became the base of No.5 Air Navigation School, which later was redesignated No.1 ANS, taking over elements of No.10 ANS at Driffield in 1949. It had Wellington T.10, Oxford T.2 and Anson T.1 aircraft on strength.

A change to Transport Command followed in 1949 with squadrons flying Hastings aircraft. However, the creation of NATO passed additional responsibility to patrol vast areas of sea to the RAF. The American-built Lockheed Neptune was ordered pending delivery of Avro Shackletons. The Neptune MR.1 was a twin-engined aircraft. Topcliffe was selected as the main base because the sphere of operations would be the North Sea. Transferred to Coastal Command in 1952, Topcliffe had three squadrons and a special flight each equipped with

Neptune aircraft for Maritime Reconnaissance until 1957 when the squadrons disbanded their role having been replaced by Avro Shackleton units in Scotland.

Topcliffe returned to Flying Training Command and No.1 ANS was reformed in 1957, operating the Varsity and Marathon in the navigator training role, but they moved on to Stradishall in Suffolk in 1961. The OCU at Dishforth had the use of the airfield as a Relief Landing Ground (RLG) for a few years. The Airborne Electronics and Air Engineers School had a number of large grounded aircraft such as a Comet, Shackleton and Valetta for training purposes. A small number of other RAF units utilised the station buildings until transfer to the British Army in 1972 as Alanbrooke Barracks.

From 1993, the RAF became a lodger unit and in 1995 No.1 FTS of Linton-on-Ouse made use of it as a RLG for flying Tucano training aircraft.

The Neptune MR.1 in RAF service initially kept the US Navy colour scheme of midnight blue rather than be camouflaged, similar to other RAF Coastal Command aircraft. Each squadron was allocated a code letter and WX523 wears 'L-X' of No.210 Squadron which received its Neptunes at Topcliffe early in 1953. Here it was shown off at an ROC day at nearby Linton-on-Ouse. (BRR)

Avro York C.1 MW285 (which could have been amongst the number built at their Yeadon factory) served with No.1332 Heavy Conversion Unit at Dishforth which disbanded into No.241 OCU in 1948. Coded 'YY-M', it seems to be parked outside the southernmost of the Dishforth Type 'C' hangars. (RCS)

No.241 OCU at Dishforth trained crews for the long-range transport squadrons and received a number of Handley Page Hastings from the first production batch. TG608 is in the original colour scheme as 'H' of No.241 OCU, seen above visiting Middleton St George in 1950. (RCS)

Vickers Valetta C.1 VW146 joined No.242 OCU at Dishforth in 1955 and coded 'NU-Z', also wearing the personalised coloured diamond then popular in Transport Command with the unit title painted across it. The last three of the aircraft serial was also painted across the tail of Transport Command aircraft. Photographed in 1957. (RCS)

Valetta C. VW190 served with No.30 Squadron at Dishforth, photographed on 24 March 1957 wearing the diamond of No.30 Squadron. It transferred to No.242 OCU, also at Dishforth, a month later taking up their markings and code 'NU-N' before being taken out of service and scrapped in July 1958. (PHB)

Valetta C.2 VW863 had been delivered and used by the OCUs before coming to No.30 Squadron at Dishforth in 1953. It remained with the squadron and took on its diamond markings until 1957. The aircraft was later posted to overseas service in the Middle East. (RCS)

This Scottish Aviation Pioneer CC.1 XL703 'Z' belonged to No.230 Squadron, based at Dishforth, and was used for army support and communications duties. The squadron spent a short time in Cyprus before returning to Dishforth in April 1959 then making a permanent move to Netheravon that year. It is seen above at Benson during a Battle of Britain display after the squadron had moved from Dishforth. The aircraft was eventually preserved for museum display, being located at the Manchester Museum of Science & Industry, but is now displayed at the Royal Air Force Museum Cosford. (RCS)

Staff aircrew of No.1 ANS, Topcliffe, posing in front of Wellington T.10 'Q'. From left to right: S2 Ken Smith; Flt Lt Don Thieme, the flight commander; P2 Dennis Lloyd; S2 Tony Leaworthy and S1 Jock McGregor. At this time the new NCO aircrew ranks, such as Signaller 2 and Pilot 2, were in force but were replaced by a further revision in the structure in 1950. Many of the aircraft and staff came from RAF Driffield when that unit disbanded. (DM)

Another but less informal photograph which shows the faired-over front turret of the Wellington T.10 and also another Wellington of the school at Topcliffe with the four-letter Flying Training Command codes on a yellow rectangle. (DM)

No. 1. AIR NAVIGATION SCHOOL. TOPCLIFFE.

The RAF was operating on a much reduced basis by 1947 and this may represent the whole of No.1 ANS training staff portrayed outside a Type 'C' hangar at Topcliffe. (DM)

Avro Ansons (and the Vickers Wellingtons) remained equipped with the standard radios and receivers as used during the Second World War for training signallers and navigators. The cramped 'office' working space is evident. (DM)

Like other Coastal Command aircraft the Neptune wore the port side code in reverse to starboard side but, additionally, the individual aircraft code is repeated on the nose. Neptune WX514 'L-R' of 210 Squadron taxies past service onlookers in 1955. (RCS)

No.203 Squadron received their Neptune MR.1 aircraft at about the same time as No.210 Squadron at Topcliffe; their squadron code was the letter 'B', with aircraft 'M' and 'L' in formation over the Vale of York, 8 March 1954. Of special interest is that B-L has the extended 'stinger' tail accommodating Magnetic Anomaly Detection and the plexiglas lookout nose of the anti-submarine version but 'B-M' does not have the tail modification, retaining the turret gun. (GWY)

Another Neptune MR .1 unit at Topcliffe was No.1453 Flt, originally under the control of Fighter rather than Coastal Command. It had been involved with Airborne Early Warning Trials over the North Sea. Not allocated a unit code, the flight used numbers to identify individual aircraft and WX500, one of the early aircraft of the batch complete with fore and aft armament, is simply '3'. (RCS)

It would seem the entire complement of all the Neptune units at Topcliffe is lined up facing the hangars. Some aircraft are in midnight blue, others in Coastal Command grey, but the squadron number of the nearest aircraft is painted in yellow. This is a view prepared for a Christmas card, c.1956. (Brian Latham via GWY)

Patrol flights went up to the Norwegian coast and often crews called in at Norwegian bases as this one did in September 1954. This was part of Exercise Morning Mist (Arctic Mist phase). The crew on this occasion was ten but eight are pictured. From left to right, back row: -?-; Flg-Off. J. Morgan (Navigator); Flt Lt J. Baker (Captain); -?-; Flg-Off. F. Yeoman (Second Pilot); Flg-Off. Seagrave (Navigator). Front row: -?-; Sgt M. Hudson (Signaller). The twin nose guns noted and individual aircraft is WX521 'L' of No.203 Squadron. (GWY)

After the Neptunes left, No.1 Air Navigation School was reformed and it took on strength a number of Miles Marathons, which had been surplus to civil requirements. One in 1958 coded 'F', serial unknown, is outside a Type 'C' hangar which shows the lower roof height and replacement of the brick or concrete cladding found on the mid-1930s expansion stations by sheeting. No.1 ANS moved to Stradishall in 1961. (DN)

The War Office took responsibility for the new Army Air Corps on 1 September 1957 and slowly built up its force. The de Havilland Canada Beaver AL.1, a rugged five-seat fixed wing aircraft, was bought. Some forty-two aircraft were built in Canada and assembled at the Hawker Siddeley works at Broughton near Chester. Two of these aircraft from No.667 Squadron AAC attended the Vale of York air show at Topcliffe and XP775 was photographed on 4 July 1971.

The Army Air Corps became a helicopter force with small units supporting various Army formations. The Westland Scout AH.1, XR628 'B' of No.666 Squadron was used to support 24th Brigade in the UK at the time. To the side is a Westland Sioux XT5666 helicopter of the same squadron, coded 'T'. Photographed 4 July 1971.

The Air Electronics School, later becoming the Air Electronics and Air Engineer School, was based at Topcliffe until its work was absorbed by No.6 FTS at Finningley, October 1973. This Varsity T.1 WJ897 'E' of the AEAES was displayed on 9 July 1972.

No.1 FTS at nearby Linton-on-Ouse had a display team called 'The Blades' with the Jet Provost T.5. XW299 '56' was at the Topcliffe display on 9 July 1972.

Being inspected by ROC Personnel on 9 July 1972 is Jodel D.117 G-AYKT, a French-built light aircraft imported into the UK during 1970, it was hangared at Topcliffe on a temporary basis. In the background is Beverley XB259, now preserved.

The Central Flying School Tucano element, parented by No.1 FTS at Linton-on-Ouse, moved to Topcliffe in April 1995 along with the Tucano navigational element of No.6 FTS Finningley when that unit disbanded. This aircraft (ZF245) wearing the CFS emblem below the cockpit was in store at RAF Shawbury during the early part of 1999; essential maintenance was being carried out.

Three
Military Airfields: Linton-on-Ouse & Church Fenton

Linton-on-Ouse

Selected under expansion scheme C with a range of Type C hangars and opened on 13 May 1937, Linton-on-Ouse began receiving the headquarters staff of No.4 Group Bomber Command and in April 1938 the first two squadrons (Nos 51 and 58) were equipped with Armstrong Whitworth Whitleys. Throughout the war, Bomber Command squadrons, later using Halifaxes, operated from Linton-on-Ouse. The Canadian squadrons in No.6 Group took over with Wellingtons, Halifaxes and, at the end, Lancasters.

Runways had been built in 1942 to 1943. As the accommodation was good, Linton was scheduled for retention and transferred to Fighter Command in 1946 as the Yorkshire (later Northern) Sector operated with Church Fenton. Nos 64 and 65 (East India) Squadrons, equipped with de Havilland Hornets, were posted to Linton 1946. No.264 (Madras Presidency) Squadron with Mosquito NF.36 was based there for a while (the squadron returned in 1951) and in October 1949 Nos 66 and 92 (East India) Squadrons were based there. In 1951 Nos 64 and 65 (F) Squadrons moved temporarily to Coltishall in Norfolk and converted to the Gloster Meteor and later relocated to Duxford in Cambridgeshire. Nos 66 and 92 had Gloster Meteors, North American Sabres and finally Hawker Hunters at Linton. No.264 (Madras Presidency) Squadron had Meteor Night Fighters until 1957 when Linton was placed on a Care & Maintenance basis. The station was readied for Flying Training Command and No.1 FTS moved in from Syerston, Nottinghamshire, with de Havilland Vampire T.11 aircraft. In 1961 the *ab initio* Jet Provost came to No.1 FTS and remained with later improved versions until replaced by the propeller-driven but efficient Shorts Tucano. Responsibility for training naval pilots was allocated to No.1 FTS. A number of local airfields, such as Full Sutton (1957/1959), Rufforth (1959/1966), Holme-on-Spalding Moor (1962/1966), Dishforth (1962), Elvington (1966), and later Church Fenton and Topcliffe, were used as RLGs. Yorkshire Universities Air Squadron and No.9AEF of Church Fenton used Linton as its operating base.

In 1968 the station was granted the Freedom of the City of York, and a fly-past lead by Squadron Ldr R.E.Turner over the City with Jet Provost T.3 and T.4 was undertaken on 24 April. Linton remains a very busy station with No.1 FTS flying the Tucano, taking over aircraft of the Central Flying School element and No.6 FTS at Finningley when they disbanded.

Church Fenton

Church Fenton was in the first pre-war expansion scheme A for Home Defence aerodromes, a scheme succeeded by others, and it was finally opened in June 1937 as a grass aerodrome with plans for two Type 'C' hangars and provision for a third. These hangars were shorter versions of the type found on Yorkshire bomber stations because of the difference in size of the aircraft to be accommodated. Construction was not completed until 1939 and runways were built shortly afterwards.

The first two fighter squadrons were No.72 (F) Squadron arriving on 1 June 1937 equipped with Gloster Gladiator biplane fighters, which were replaced by Spitfires in April 1939, and No.213 (F) Squadron a month later with an earlier Gloster fighter, the Gauntlet. No.213 (F) Squadron was replaced by No.64 (F) Squadron in May 1938, again with biplane fighters, the Hawker Demon and then by a fighter version of the Bristol Blenheim. Upon the outbreak of war, most squadrons switched bases, and Church Fenton became an important fighter base for the defence of the area. In late 1940 No.54 Operational Training Unit was formed with the purpose of training night fighter crews and they remained until mid-1942 when the day and night fighter squadrons returned, each spending a short time with No.25 Squadron, being in residence for night fighter protection of the area for about eighteen months.

At the end of the war, Church Fenton was retained as an important fighter sector station, housing both day and night fighters until a complete reorganisation of Britain's defence was carried out in the late 1950s and squadrons were either disbanded or moved to other stations. During this time, like Linton-on-Ouse, it housed a Hornet Day Fighter wing, these aircraft being replaced by Gloster Meteors, including the Night Fighter role and Hunters with Javelins for a short period. The role of Church Fenton then changed, housing a number of second line units and Leeds University Air Squadron/No.9 Air Experience Flight, until becoming a Jet Provost training station when No.7 FTS was reformed in 1962. Later in that decade, the training role changed and the Primary Training Squadron of the Central Flying School equipped with de Havilland Chipmunks took over. They were succeeded by No.2 FTS with Chipmunks and Bulldogs, then No.7 FTS reformed again using Jet Provosts until they disbanded in 1992. Elvington in 1962, 1966 and 1979, and Rufforth in 1970 were used by the various based schools as RLGs. Throughout the last thirty years or so, Church Fenton has been used as a RLG by No.1 FTS at Linton-on-Ouse and other training units.

Church Fenton, 9 April 2002. Civilian-operated Slingsby T-67M Firefly trainer G-BWXU of the Joint Elementary Flying Training School based at Barkston Heath in Lincolnshire. It uses Church Fenton as an outstation.

No.64 (F) Squadron was the first RAF squadron to receive the de Havilland Hornet, a fast single-seat fighter, in May 1946. The squadron moved to Linton-on-Ouse in August 1946 to form one part of the Linton-on-Ouse Wing with No.65 (East India) Squadron also flying Hornets. It refuelled with 100 octane contained in a 450 gallon trailer bowser towed by a tractor, arrangements similar to practice during the Second World War. Hornet F.1 PX241 SH-N carries the revised British nationality markings which omitted the white part of the roundel and fin flash. (RAF Linton-on-Ouse)

A group of No.64 (F) Squadron pilots whilst at the Acklington Armament Practice Camp in 1949. The variety of uniforms and the attached USAF pilot are interesting. In addition to regular air exercises involving interception of high flying bombers over the UK, live practice firing air to air and air to ground was carried out over ranges from RAF Acklington in Northumberland. (RAF Linton-on-Ouse)

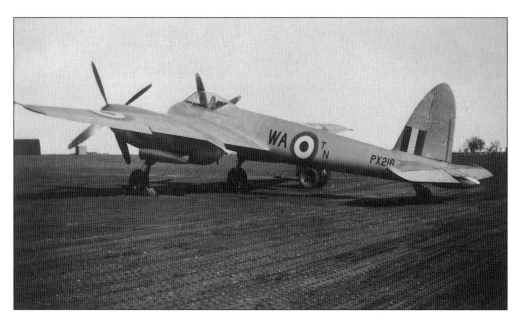

The Linton Hornet Wing was commanded by Wg Cdr W.A. 'Tiny' Neale who had his personal markings applied to this Hornet F.1 PX216 as 'WA-TN'. Before delivery to HQ Yorkshire Sector, Linton-on-Ouse, this aircraft had been involved in photographic reconnaissance development work. (S/L D. Hyams via RCS)

The sister squadron to No.64 in the Linton-on-Ouse Hornet Wing was No.65 (East India) Squadron. The Linton Hornet squadrons were re-equipped with the F.3 version in 1948 which had increased range and attachment points for rocket projectiles. A dorsal fin was added to improve rudder and directional characteristics. This Hornet F.3 PX362 'YT-L' (also YT-C at one time) has the squadron device of a 'lion passant' on the fin, the aircraft showed rogue characteristics and it was returned to de Havilland Aircraft Co. Ltd for investigation. (RCS)

No.66 (F) Squadron received the Gloster Meteor F.4 in 1948 and moved to Linton in 1949. Their aircraft were in a silver colour scheme and wore squadron codes not visible in this photograph; the nearest aircraft (VT139) has some form of insignia below the cockpit. (RAF Linton-on-Ouse)

By the end of 1950, both No.66 and 92 (F) Squadrons at Linton had re-equipped with the Meteor F.8 and also acquired squadron markings in lieu of codes. These Meteor F.8s carry No.92's red and yellow checkerboard either side of the fuselage roundel at a 1951 ROC Day, Linton-on-Ouse. (BRR Collection/BHA)

The Hawker Hunter F.4 code 'E' of No.66 (F) Squadron at Linton-on-Ouse with others of the squadron await departure from the Aircraft Servicing Platform in front of the hangars. This mark of the Hunter remained in service until about October 1956 when it was replaced with the F.6, which had improved flying controls and a more powerful engine. (RAF Linton-on-Ouse)

The American-designed North American Sabre was obtained by the RAF in substantial numbers, mainly for service with Second Tactical Air Force in Germany. However, two squadrons in Fighter Command, both based at Linton-on-Ouse, used the type between the Meteor and Hunter coming into service. Sabre F.4 XD735 'T' of No.66 (F) Squadron in camouflage forms the backdrop to 'Chunky' Ianson and Ira Fothergill in 1954. (*Yorkshire Post*)

No.66 (F) Squadron started to receive the Hawker Hunter F.4 in March 1956. This photograph, taken some time later, shows the change in squadron markings and they held on to at least one Sabre! Nearest aircraft is Hunter F.4 WV409 'N' with the squadron marking and badge displayed below the cockpit. Next is the Sabre F.4 XD753, without an individual code but special marking suggesting use by a senior officer, and a Meteor F.8 WK656 'S'; both have the white rectangle on either side of the fuselage roundel outlined in blue. All aircraft now wear the standard day fighter camouflage. (RAF Linton-on-Ouse)

Most squadrons had a number of Meteor T.7 aircraft for various duties. No.66 (F) Squadron had VZ630 'Z' in a silver colour scheme with yellow training bands and their squadron markings, which consisted of a white rectangle outlined top and bottom in blue. The C Type hangar to the rear has a good growth of trees, originally planted to help camouflage the building. (LPR)

No.92 (East India) Squadron Hunter F.6s, received in February 1957 to replace the F.4s, lined up at the northern end of the Linton Aircraft Servicing Platform. Their red and yellow checkerboard displayed on XG211 'H', this aircraft after RAF service found itself exported to the Indian Air Force. (RAF Linton-on-Ouse)

A formation of Hunter F.6s of No.92 (East India) Squadron: XG233 'J', XG237 'G', XG226 'D' and XG229 'F'. The squadron moved to Middleton St George in March 1957 and in 1961-1962, whilst based at Leconfield, were the official RAF Display Team 'The Blue Diamonds'. (RAF Linton-on-Ouse)

No.1 FTS at Linton-on-Ouse received the Hunting Provost T.3 and T.4 (a more powerful version suited for higher altitude training). However, the T.4s left service before the T.3, which continued to be used after the totally revised T.5 came into service. XM472 '22' is seen above in one of the 'C' Type hangars on 28 October 1981.

Jet Provost T.3A XN589 '46' in service with No.1 FTS on 28 October 1981 was obtained for gate guarding duties located by the main entrance. With the exception of the addition of the unit badge, the markings are unaltered.

When the British Aircraft Corporation took over Hunting Aircraft, the Jet Provost was further developed at Warton producing the T.5 version, ordered in quantity by the RAF. No.1 FTS operated a sizeable fleet of this mark at Linton including XW327 '62' on 28 October 1981. Apart from the unit designation on the fin, the school crest is carried below the cockpit.

To celebrate seventy-five years of No.1 FTS, at least two Tucanos carried special markings. ZF408 is illustrated at the Finningley Air Day, 17 September 1994. The second Tucano marked was ZF514.

Linton Gate Guardian Percival Provost T.1 XF545 'O-K' on 28 October 1981commemorates the days that No.1 FTS was equipped with the type when it was used simultaneously with the Vampire T.11. This particular aircraft never flew with No.1 FTS but it had been selected for the RAF Museum Regional Collection and kept for ten years at Finningley, exhibited as 'P-Z' and 7975M (a type of serial allocated to all grounded aircraft used for instructional or display purposes). Eventually, it found its way to Linton and wears the standard colour scheme with markings of No.6 FTS, appropriate to the time the school was based at Tern Hill in Shropshire.

A general view of the Memorial Room at Linton which is a tribute to those who have served at the station. Many contributions have been received from former personnel; the staff who have assembled and managed the collection are to be complimented.

The control tower now known as the Air Traffic Control building was originally erected at Linton-on-Ouse in about 1939 (Air Ministry drawing 5845/39), officially known as a Watch Office with Meteorological Section. It replaced a smaller building of a 1936 design as there was a need to accommodate more facilities. Over the years it has been updated, especially with the construction of a Visual Control Room and a new fire escape to comply with the latest safety regulations. Equipped with good radar equipment, Air Traffic Control can look after all the local operations of No.1 FTS and monitor air activity in the region.

Tucanos of No.1 FTS on the main apron at Linton-on-Ouse in 1995. The colour scheme of red and white is slowly being replaced by an all-black scheme with national markings having better day visibility characteristics. (LM)

No.19(F) Squadron arrived at Church Fenton in April 1947 from Wittering where it had re-equipped with the de Havilland Hornet F.1; these were exchanged for the F.3 in May 1948. Hornet F.3 PX293 'QV-A' served with No.19(F) Squadron between late 1947 and spring 1951. (Peter Green via RCS)

No.19 (F) Squadron received the Meteor F.4 in 1951 at Church Fenton then the F.8 version, until replaced by the Hunters and the subsequent move to Leconfield. This line up of No.19 (F) Squadron Meteor F.8s with air and ground crews shows the blue and white checkerboard marking with the COs aircraft WE863 having it repeated on the fin. Many of the ground crew personnel were National Servicemen. The squadron Meteor T.7 lurks in the background. (BJ/*Aeroplane Monthly*)

A Royal Observer Corps day at Church Fenton on 19 August 1956 brought this Hunter F.4 WV314 belonging to No.92(East India) Squadron as 'B', normally based at Linton-on-Ouse. (Stan Hall via NS)

No.85 Squadron moved from West Malling in Kent to Church Fenton during September 1957 until disbandment on 31 October 1958. Armstrong Whitworth Meteor NF.14 WS744 served with them, red and black checkerboard squadron markings on either side of the fuselage roundel noted. (RAF Linton-on-Ouse)

Gloster Javelin F(AW).1 XA568 was one of the first aircraft of the type delivered to an RAF squadron, No.46 Squadron at Odiham, Hampshire, early in 1956. Coded 'J' but with the absence of any squadron markings, XA568 was brought to the ROC day at Church Fenton on 19 August 1956. (Stan Hall via NS)

Avro Anson PH782 was built as a C.12 in 1945 at Yeadon for communications and light transport duties. By 1956 it had most recently served with the Fighter Command Communications Squadron at Bovingdon and the Armament Practice Camp at Acklington in Northumberland. It is seen here at Church Fenton being refuelled in 1956, the shorter version the 'C' type hangar for the pre-war expansion fighter stations is evident. The aircraft was written off in a take-off accident at Acklington on 14 November 1956. (HH)

Appearing at the SSAFA display Church Fenton 3 June 1963 was Beverley XM105 'P' of No.47 Squadron, based at Abingdon in Oxfordshire. The runway control van painted in orange and white squares is parked by the hangar.

The Leeds University Air Squadron (later merged to be part of the Yorkshire Universities Air Squadron) has spent most of its time based at Church Fenton, during 1962-1963 at Dishforth, but sent Chipmunk T.10 WG316 to the SSAFA display on 3 June 1963. Coloured quarters in a square denote the University identity . This aircraft was civilianised in 1974 and by 1988 was based at Shoreham whilst officially registered as G-BCAH, flies in its military markings. Chipmunks saw extensive use by No.2 FTS at Church Fenton from 1970.

Gate guard at Church Fenton was Meteor NF(T).14 WS739 on 20 October 1973. It has been given the squadron marking of No.85 Squadron which operated the type at Church Fenton between 1957 and 1958. This particular aircraft didn't serve with No.85 Squadron but was previously used training, hence the silver colour scheme instead of camouflage. (NS)

Being filmed in Yorkshire during the early part of 1981 was the television series about a fictional airline called Ruskin Air Services. A number of civil Douglas Dakotas were painted up in period markings and 'G-AGHY' appeared at the Church Fenton SSAFA display on 14 June 1981. Church Fenton was used for many of the flying sequences.

The Church Fenton SSAFA display grew enormously in stature and attracted many NATO visitors, including this Fairchild A-10 'Tank Buster' aircraft of the United States Air Force based at Wethersfield in Essex. These aircraft flying at low level in specially designated areas were a familiar sight in Yorkshire, Derbyshire, Lincolnshire and Eastern England for many years.

An exotic visitor was this Lockheed P-5 Orion of the US Navy to SSAFA, 13 June 1982.

Differences between the Jet Provost T.3/ 4 and T.5 like XW320 of No.7 FTS show the much improved cockpit area on 13 June 1982. The Church Fenton emblem and number code do not mean that the school had at least 120 aircraft on strength!

Six of the ever popular Red Arrows official RAF Display Team awaiting their turn at SSAFA, 13 June 1982. Church Fenton had the shorter version of the familiar 'C' Type hangar found on the permanent stations of the RAF in Yorkshire.

Scottish Aviation Bulldog T.1 XX621 'D' of the Yorkshire Universities Air Squadron, based at Finningley, attended the SSAFA Church Fenton air show on 13 June 1982. It also carries the squadron marking of an opened book on a blue square. A North American Rockwell OV-10 Bronco ground attack aircraft of the USAF was also in the static display.

The Jet Provost T. 3 remained in service, as shown by XM465 '85' of No.7 FTS at the SSAFA display on 13 June 1982. Behind the aircraft is a pair of United States Air Force Fairchild A-10 'tank busters'.

Left: Special attention was given to the architectural and ornamental appearance of the pre-war RAF expansion stations like Church Fenton. The Main Gates at Church Fenton are a particularly good example, making a most pleasing effect on entering at what was once a principal airfield in the defence of Britain, 8 September 2001.

Below: A charming well-maintained village sign has been built between the RAF Station and the village. A Spitfire is depicted as a reminder of the squadrons which used the type from Church Fenton, 8 September 2001.

Four
Military Airfields: Leconfield & Driffield

RAF Leconfield

With expansion scheme C approved on 21 May 1936, construction at Leconfield commenced, expecting to be ready for full occupation by 5 November 1936. Delays meant the first units scheduled, Nos 10 and 78 (Bomber) Squadrons, were re-allocated to Dishforth. Five large Type 'C' hangars were erected fronting a grass aerodrome with all the supporting station buildings. By the beginning of 1937 Leconfield was ready to receive two squadrons, Nos 97 and 166, which had Handley Page Heyford bombers, replaced by Whitleys. In 1938 both squadrons were designated as training squadrons for No.4 (B) Group, Bomber Command.

The squadrons moved out upon outbreak of war and Leconfield was placed on a Care & Maintenance basis pending Fighter Command taking over, rotating squadrons in the defence of the East Yorkshire area. By the end of 1941, No.4 (B) Group returned and hard runways with dispersals built for the resumption of bombing operations. No.4 Group was transferred to Transport Command in 1945 and vacated the station in the middle of the year since Leconfield was to be the new home of the Central Gunnery School (later Fighter Weapons School), previously at Catfoss.

By the late 1950s there was a need for another fighter base nearer the coast and Leconfield received the Church Fenton squadrons and also one from Middleton St George. No.92 Squadron, whilst based at Leconfield, was the official RAF Display Team 'The Blue Diamonds' in 1961-1962. Policy changed and in the mid-1960s Leconfield was engaged in servicing RAF aircraft until closed and handed over to Army on 1 January 1977, re-named Normandy Barracks with a satellite at Driffield (airfield site). Leconfield was then used by the Army School of Mechanical Transport later becoming the Defence School of Transport for all three services.

An RAF enclave still remains at Leconfield as a lodger unit operating helicopters in the air-sea rescue role.

RAF Driffield

Driffield has one of the most interesting and varied histories of all Yorkshire airfields. As early as 1917 a properly developed aerodrome for training had been established when Driffield was known as Eastburn. At the close of the First World War the name had given way to Driffield but the aerodrome was not retained and the buildings removed.

The search for new bomber airfields brought attention to the Driffield site under expansion scheme C. In August 1936 the first two squadrons Nos 58 and 215 arrived with Vickers

Virginias, a rather ancient and obsolete bomber. Five large steel framed but concrete clad hangars Type 'C' were still in the process of erection and the station buildings mainly contained in huts. As building progressed, more permanent station quarters of concrete and brick construction were built. Bomber squadrons in No.4 (B) Group rotated and more modern types were seen at Driffield so that by the outbreak of war in September 1939, Armstrong Whitworth Whitley's were in service. Driffield suffered a major enemy air attack in August 1940 leading to a reorganisation of the operating units. During rebuilding the grass runways gave way to hard runways and dispersals with bomber squadrons in residence until the end of the war.

When the No.4 Group squadrons, now in Transport Command, left, Driffield came within Flying Training Command. Units including the first RAF Meteor equipped the No.203 Advanced Flying School. Extensive use was made of Carnaby, the wartime emergency landing runway. In the mid to late 1950s, Driffield housed two night fighter squadrons but with the next major change into the missile age, in the role as the main base of five Thor Intermediate Range Ballistic Missile squadrons, Driffield had its own squadron with others located at Full Sutton, Breighton, Catfoss and Carnaby.

After the Thor missile units were disbanded in 1963, the airfield and camp site was used for a variety of purposes although not by flying units other than Hawker Siddeley Aviation Ltd for some Buccaneer work. The airfield area is used by the driving school at Leconfield and the station buildings one-time Staxton Wold Camp, Driffield and Alamein Barracks still remain; their future is uncertain.

No.19 (F) Squadron relocated from Church Fenton to Leconfield on 29 June 1959 with its Hawker Hunter F.6s. The Battle of Britain day on 17 September 1960 gave an opportunity to see them. This unidentified aircraft, coded 'J', has the squadron checkerboard on each side of the fuselage roundels and also a small representation of the squadron badge below the cockpit. (HH)

Spitfire LF.XVIe RW382 marked as M7245, its Maintenance Command serial, and 3L-Q of the RAF Fighter Command Control and Reporting School of Middle Wallop in Hampshire stood at Leconfield from 1959. It was required for the *Battle of Britain* film in 1968, thereafter going to RAF Uxbridge; there it was replaced by a 'plastic' Spitfire and in 1988 sold to a civil company for restoration to flying condition. Still carrying RAF markings as RW382, the code 'NG-C' was applied to represent its earlier service with No.604 (County of Middlesex) Squadron RAuxAF based at North Weald in Essex after the war. The aircraft was exported to the United States in 1995.

No.72 (Basutoland) Squadron relocated from Church Fenton to Leconfield on 28 June 1959. It had just re-equipped with the Gloster Javelin F(AW).4. On the huge Javelin fin, 'H' XA755 displays the squadron emblem, a 'Swift Volant', on a disc, 17 September 1960. The squadron disbanded at Leconfield on 30 June 1961. (HH)

Most RAF stations were equipped with 'hack' aircraft used for a variety of purposes. Gloster Meteor F.8 (TT) WK817 '2' of the Leconfield Station Flight was used to tow sleeve targets in order that the squadrons could practice live air firing over designated areas. Aircraft was allocated to No.19 and 72 squadrons, 3 September 1960.

Hunter F.6 XG185 'T' of No.19 (F) Squadron, 17 September 1960. (HH)

No.19 (F) Squadron gave up their Hunters in November 1962 in favour of their new mounts the BAC Lightning F.2 which they continued to fly from Leconfield until the squadron was posted to Gutersloh in Germany on 23 September 1965. Lightning XN778 'F' of No.19 (F) Squadron seen at the Waddington, Lincolnshire Battle of Britain display, 19 September 1964. The squadron emblem of a 'dolphins head between wings' is on the fin.

Air Anglia operated regular services through Leeds Bradford Airport and started a scheduled service in 1973 between Hull and Jersey in the Channel Islands. The RAF aerodrome at Leconfield needed to be used and this Fokker F-27 Friendship G-BCDN (the third delivered to the airline) at Leconfield in September 1975. No customs facilities were available at Leconfield so services had to be flown via Castle Donington (East Midlands Airport) or Norwich Airport to clear customs, this route being eventually abandoned. The airline was later known as Air UK and now KLM UK. (NS)

The Leconfield Control Tower (now used by the Army for administration purposes) was originally similar to the one at Catterick as illustrated but built of concrete (Air Ministry drawing 207/36). However, the 'tower' was later removed and replaced with a control room as a new upper storey. Additional accommodation was necessary when Leconfield became an important fighter airfield with the result that a large extension was built with a new Visual Control Room, 15 September 1999.

The Westland Sea King has been the principal RAF rescue aircraft now for many years. No.202 Squadron has a number of flights stationed at coastal airfields and Leconfield is the base of 'E' Flight which, on 15 September 1999, was operating XZ588.

No.204 Advanced Flying School was based at Driffield (March 1948 to August 1949) with Mosquito T.3 and FB.6 providing advanced training prior to crews going to other units, such as No.228 Operational Conversion Unit at Leeming. No.121 Course (6 September 1948 to 29 December 1948) from left to right, standing: -?- ; Flt Lt 'Rolly' Duck (Navigator); Nav IV Readings; -?- . Seated: Pilot IV Patching, Flt Lt Trevor Barlow-Jones; P/O Iain Dick and Pilot IV Bickerton. (ID)

Mosquito FB.6 flown at Driffield with No.204 AFS is SZ973 carrying the Flying Training Command Codes 'FMO-S', presented in the style to identify the unit code 'FMO'. Aircraft painted silver with yellow training bands may denote a change in configuration. (ID)

No.203 AFS reformed at Driffield in September 1949 and being the first school of its type with jet-powered aircraft received a lot of attention. This line-up of Gloster Meteor F.4 (single seat) and T.7 (two seat) is on the 'grass' outside the hangar line as the new concrete aircraft apron had not then been built. Unit codes 'FMJ' (Meteor F.4) and 'FMK' (Meteor T.7) are applied, reading the opposite on the starboard side. In the distance can be seen a de Havilland Vampire (codes 'FMI') which was also on the school strength for a different type of advanced training. (BJ/*Aeroplane Monthly*)

Pilots destined for the ground attack role in the RAF received training at No.203 AFS, Driffield initially on the two-seat Meteor T.7 for jet experience and then going onto the Vampire F.1 – there wasn't a two-seat version of the Vampire at the time. This group of pilots on No.2 Vampire Course in December 1949, from left to right, back row: P/O Waudby; P/O Richardson; P III Vilaies. Front row: P/O Walker; P/O Taylor; Pilot II Chappell; Pilot I Reid and Pilot IV Stuart. (JS)

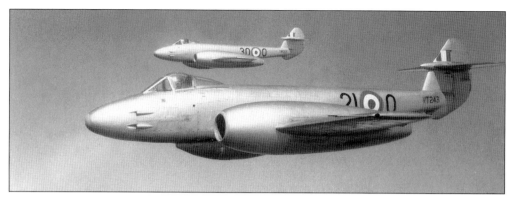

By 1952 the format of Flying Training Command codes had changed to a simple letter and number system. Formation flying was an important part of the syllabus and these Meteor F.4 VT243 O-21 and VW 266 O-30 were photographed June/July 1952. Both survived the rigours of school flying to be converted to unmanned aircraft for missile trials. (DD)

A mix of Meteor F.4 and T.7s are in this formation with T.7 WG964 nearest, coded X-66. (BHA Collection)

No.33 Squadron along with No.219 Squadron reformed at Driffield in 1955 and provided night fighter defence of the area up to the mid-1957 when both were disbanded. The de Havilland Venom NF.2A formed the equipment and WR783 from No.33 Squadron appeared at the Burtonwood Armed Forces day in 1957.

After the night fighter squadrons were disbanded, Driffield was used by the Fighter Command Modification Centre and Gloster Javelin F(AW).6 XA819 was recorded in March 1958 prior to issue to No.29 Squadron at Acklington. (JK)

The Fighter Weapons School based at nearby Leconfield moved over to Driffield in 1957 until absorbed by the Central Fighter Establishment. Driffield was then vacated by flying units. This Hawker Hunter WT739 in use by the FWS 'E' had the distinction of previously being on the strength of No.111 Squadron (The Black Arrows) and used by its C.O. Sqdn Ldr Roger Topp to break the air speed record between London and Edinburgh. (JK)

De Havilland Vampire T.11 WZ547 was used by the FWS at Driffield until the school was posted away in 1958 as part of the CFE. (JK)

Driffield had the conventional five aircraft sheds or, as they are better known, hangars; two for each squadron and a repair shed. One was totally destroyed during the August 1940 air raid but the others were repaired and continued to be used right up to the present time. Driffield's Type 'C' were steel-framed and clad in concrete with massive steel doors at either end (Air Ministry drawing 3264/35). The hangars were substantially modified after the RAF left to be used as grain stores. Building No.64 (Hangar No.3) has all the glazing replaced including the annexes which had been used as squadron offices etc. Photographed on 5 January 1999. (GS)

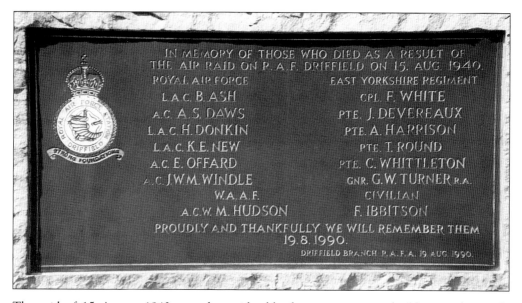

The raid of 15 August 1940 caused considerable damage to station buildings and aircraft. Unfortunately a number of servicemen and women lost their lives and a memorial located in front of the Station Headquarters was dedicated on 19 August 1990. (GS)

Left: Familiar to many airmen who have passed through these and reported to the adjacent Guardroom. The brick pillars carry the 'star' device (cast in concrete) as part of the pre-war expansion period of decoration, September 1999.

Below: When more substantial domestic accommodation was erected at Driffield, replacing the temporary wooden huts, these were of brick construction to standard Air Ministry drawing 1723-4/36, similar to other expansion period airfields. They are seen here in use for the camp administration, 7 September 2001.

Five
Military Airfields: Finningley & Lindholme

Finningley

Finningley was planned under RAF expansion Scheme C as a bomber station, compulsory purchase of land taking place in September 1935 with construction starting almost immediately. An advance party arrived on 30 July 1936, initially for No.3 Group squadrons; the first aircraft arrived on 31 August 1936. Nos 102 and 7 (Bomber) Squadrons were posted in on 3 September 1936, the date of official opening. Shortly afterwards, No.4 Group which controlled most of the Yorkshire airfields took over until early in 1939 when Finningley was transferred to No.5 Group. Upon outbreak of war, operations commenced but from 1941 Finningley was used by night bomber Operational Training Units through to the end of the war. Rebuilding with hard runways took place from November 1943 to May 1944.

RAF Flying Training Command took over during the years 1947 to 1954. In May Finningley was closed again until May 1957 for complete rebuilding as 'V' Bomber base. The runway was relaid and considerably lengthened; new dispersals constructed with specialised nuclear weapons stores were prepared. No.616 (South Yorkshire) Squadron Royal Auxiliary Air Force, which had reformed at Finningley in 1946, moved out to Worksop in 1955 where it remained until disbandment in 1957. Avro Vulcans of No.101 Squadron were based at Finningley in the nuclear role from 1957 in No.1 Group, joined by Vickers Valiants of No.18 Squadron with specialist radio countermeasure equipment. The Bomber Command Development Unit was also based between 1960 and 1968. In 1961 the Vulcans of No.101 Squadron moved to Waddington in Lincolnshire exchanging places with No.230 OCU, also equipped with Vulcans in the crew training role. No.18 Squadron was disbanded when the Valiant was taken out of service in 1963.

A reduction in Britain's nuclear forces involved No.230 OCU moving to Scampton and Finningley being taken over by Training/Support Command No.23 Group in 1970. No.6 FTS specialising in training navigators was reformed at Finningley on 6 May 1970 and, for the next twenty five years, the principal flying unit operated from Finningley. Centralised maintenance for the helicopters of the ASR squadrons (No.22 and 202) was provided and in 1993 No.100 Squadron, with BAe Hawks providing target facilities, arrived. The Yorkshire Universities Air Squadron/No.9 Air Experience Flight was based there between 1975 and 1995.

Finningley closed down as an RAF base in 1996 and plans continue for its development as a civil airport.

Lindholme

Lindholme came under the later expansion scheme M as Hatfield Woodhouse (renamed Lindholme on 18 August 1940). It opened on 1 June 1940 in No.5 (Bomber) Group Bomber Command with No.50 (Bomber) Squadron arriving from Waddington with Handley Page Hampdens. Because of the geographical location, the airfield came under the bomber groups in North Lincolnshire. Canadian and Polish bomber squadrons were based with the station then going into No.1 (Bomber) Group. Two runways and dispersals were built between July and October 1942. Training units also occupied the station and at the end of the war it was scheduled for retention still in Bomber Command.

Lindholme began its association with the Avro Lincoln in 1946 with operational squadrons, No.230 OCU and the Bomber Command Bombing School over the next several years. The nearby bombing range at Misson provided facilities as well as the ranges off the Lincolnshire coast. The School was later known as the Strike Command Bombing School. Lindholme also controlled and provided servicing facilities for the Bloodhound missile squadrons at Misson, Breighton and Carnaby which were protecting the bases in the area. The SCBS now equipped with Varsities and Hastings moved to Scampton in 1972. After lying unused, Lindholme was used as a RLG by No.6 FTS Finningley between 1978 and 1985 when it was announced that the Home Office would be taking over and re-developing the site as a prison.

Representing No.616 (South Yorkshire) Squadron Royal Auxiliary Air Force based at Finningley 1951-1955, Gloster Meteor F.8 WL168 was initially painted as 'WH456' coded 'L' at Finningley in the 1970s. It moved elsewhere but returned to Finningley now painted in camouflage, squadron markings of yellow diamonds on a green rectangle, but as 'WK864' and coded 'C', 19 September 1988. When Finningley closed, the aircraft was transported by road to the Yorkshire Air Museum at Elvington and placed on exhibition.

Three Avro Vulcan B.1 provide a fly-past on 13 June 1959. No.101 Squadron (the second Vulcan squadron) had reformed at Finningley on 15 October 1957, receiving one aircraft, and crews converted to type at No.230 OCU, then based at Waddington in Lincolnshire. By April 1958, more aircraft had been received to bring its complement up to eight. Aircraft were overall in 'white anti-flash' paint. The squadron moved to Waddington in June 1961. (HH)

No.18 Squadron was reformed on 16 December 1958 at Finningley with the Valiant B.1 and remained based there until disbanded on 31 March 1963. This Valiant WZ372 did a fly-past at the September 1961 Battle of Britain 'At Home' display.

Many Avro Vulcans were converted to the B.1A version with upgraded equipment. XA907 served with the Waddington Wing then the Bomber Command Development Unit at Finningley, which had Vulcans attached from time to time. When the Vulcan went 'low level', an upper surface camouflage scheme was introduced (later extended to lower surfaces). Battle of Britain display, 19 September 1964.

Vulcan B.2 XH537 had been used for the American Skybolt underwing missile trials before joining No.230 OCU at Finningley in May 1965. It was shown in the static park at the Battle of Britain display on 17 September 1966, a Cadet glider adjacent and a USAF F-100 Super Sabre in the background.

No.6 FTS reformed at Finningley on 6 May 1970, equipped with the Vickers Varsity T.1 from the disbanded No.2 ANS at Gaydon, Warwickshire. In addition, Finningley also received some Varsities from No.5 FTS Oakington, Cambridgeshire, which had also disbanded. Varsity WF423 'P' (shown here at Gaydon, 16 September 1967) came to No.6 FTS but was destroyed in a Finningley hangar fire on 4 September 1970.

The Hawker Siddeley Dominie T.1, used by the disbanded No.1 ANS at Stradishall, Suffolk, was re-allocated to No.6 FTS and arrived in August 1970 to replace the Varsities. The type was a common sight at all the Finningley displays and XS731 'J', like the others in the fleet, hardly changed their colour schemes throughout the whole period of service.

No.22 Squadron Headquarters Flight at Finningley used the Westland Whirlwind in the Search & Rescue role and began to re-equip with the specially converted Westland Wessex as illustrated by XR518 on 17 September 1983. It wears the squadron marking of 'Maltese Cross and pi symbol' on the tail.

The Multi-Engined Training Squadron at Leeming with Scottish Aviation Jetstream T.1 joined No.6 FTS at Finningley in April 1979. On 1 June 1992, the Jetstream element of No.6 FTS was designated No.45 (Reserve) Squadron and the aircraft took up markings of the disbanded No.45 Squadron. XX491, still carrying code 'K', has a red diamond on a black stripe across the fin and a stylised 'Winged Camel' of the squadron badge below the cockpit.

The Jet Provost T.5 replaced the earlier models used by No.6 FTS in 1975; seen above at the Finningley air show day, 18 September 1993, on dispersal. They had vacated the hangars which were being used for ground displays. An emblem of the unit is above the fin flash. When both of these aircraft were taken out of service they were exported to civilian operators in the United States of America.

Freshly arrived at Finningley, No.100 Squadron had its Hawks in an overall grey scheme with a blue and yellow checkerboard across the fin. The squadron badge of a 'two human bones in satire, a skull' is represented on the nose checker board diamond. Finningley 18 September 1993.

Situated on the opposite side of the airfield to the hangar line, a new Air Traffic Control building was erected during the 1954-1957 building to a new standard design, 2548a/55, known as Vertical Split Control. Similar control towers appeared at other RAF stations and not necessarily at 'V' bomber stations. The original control tower (or watch office) was to the drawing 207/36, like other Yorkshire aerodromes of the time, was demolished. The Air Traffic Control building was mothballed in 1997.

Following the departure of the RAF in 1996-1997, various proposals have been put forward to develop the whole site, the principal one being to restructure as a civil airport and attraction of industry using surplus station buildings.

The Avro Lincoln B.2 formed the major equipment of the Bomber Command Bombing School, which moved to Lindholme from Scampton (Lincolnshire) in 1952. Lincoln RF570 served with the BCBS and both before and after service with a number of RAF bomber squadrons. (HH)

Lincoln B.2 WD143 was one of the last of its type built and served with the BCBS. Some fourteen Lincolns were seen at Lindholme during the Battle of Britain display on 19 September 1959. The School Lincolns had blue spinners and equipped with radar bomb sights to train future 'V' bomber crews.

Also used by the BCBS for training 'V' bomber crews was the Vickers Varsity T.1, WJ949 'S', seen above on 19 September 1959. It has red spinners denoting a different section of the School undertaking conventional bombing techniques. The Varsity had been designed as a bombing trainer as well as multi-engine advanced trainer.

The BCBS had evaluated the Hastings as a replacement for the Lincolns. Handley Page Hastings T.5 (converted from a C.1) TG503 was one of the first production Hastings and had been engaged in development work, including radar trials. It had ventral radar installed, necessary for the trainee 'V' bomber crews, and TG503, on the strength of the BCBS, carried no other unit markings other than red spinners on 19 September 1959.

Lindholme, opening in 1940, had the later version of the massive Type 'C' hangars and the standard concrete 'Watch Office with Meteorological Section' (control tower) to Air Ministry drawing 2328/39. The control tower was improved some time after 1955 by the addition of a large Visual Control Room and more ground floor accommodation. This view, taken whilst Lindholme was used by No.6 FTS Finningley as a RLG, shows various rescue vehicles parked outside. (BHA Collection)

Most if not all RAF airfields were clearly signed to warn unauthorised entry. Photographed in July 1984, Lindholme is quiet as, by this time, use by Finningley had declined. The later 'C' Type hangar is shown in the distance. (APF)

Six
Civil Airports

Commercial airline flying within the United Kingdom was still in its infancy at the beginning of the Second World War. A number of air services had been attempted to connect Yorkshire airports with London and continental destinations. Municipal authorities responding to the recommendations by Sir Alan Cobham began opening aerodromes with, for example, Kingston upon Hull at Hedon in 1929, Leeds and Bradford Corporations at Yeadon in 1931, at Doncaster by the famous race course in 1934 and York at Clifton in 1936.

KLM-Royal Dutch Airlines opened a service between Amsterdam and Liverpool, calling at Hedon in 1934, but later transferred the 'stop' to Doncaster. Airline operations at Yeadon in 1935 had services to various UK destinations but these were short-lived. Doncaster Airport also had a 'scheduled' service to London.

The gathering of war clouds saw the formation of squadrons in the Auxiliary Air Force. The first Yorkshire squadron – No.608 Squadron – had been formed at RAF Thornaby aerodrome. No.609 Squadron was formed at Yeadon in 1936, initially as a day bomber becoming a fighter squadron and, at Doncaster Airport, No.616 Squadron was formed in 1938 as a fighter squadron. Elementary & Reserve Flying Training Schools providing initial training for RAF pilots were formed under the aegis of the civil flying schools. At Brough, the home of the Blackburn Aircraft Ltd, the reserve flying school established in 1924 fell into this new arrangement. Outbreak of war on 3 September 1939 brought an end to civil flying until 1946 when civil operations recommenced, mainly charter work and the beginnings of club flying.

The Ministry of Civil Aviation handed Yeadon back to the Leeds and Bradford Corporations in 1953; the aerodrome had been requisitioned during the war and used mainly by A.V. Roe & Co. Ltd for the manufacture of aircraft. Air services were reinstated using the pre-war air terminal/control tower with customs facilities being introduced in 1956. Passenger handling was considerably improved by the erection of a new terminal building and control tower in 1968 on the site of the former RAF station and municipal hangar. A new runway was also built which, along with the terminal building, has been extended and improved further still over the years.

More recently, the opening of the new Sheffield Airport (one of the few new airports to be opened in the UK) and projected use of the former RAF Finningley as a new Doncaster Airport continues progress of civil aviation within the borders of the original county.

Handley Page Halton G-AJZY, belonging to the Lancashire Aircraft Corporation Ltd, at an 'Open Day' Yeadon 13 June 1948. The Halton was developed from the Halifax bomber, a type of aircraft familiar in wartime Yorkshire skies; this Halton completed 228 sorties in the Berlin Air Lift carrying food and other supplies. (D.Yeadon via GM)

A number of small airlines have been formed at Yeadon. North-South Airlines Ltd began in March 1959 with ad hoc charters using this de Havilland Heron G-ANCI. It is seen here providing pleasure flights at the Soldiers, Sailors and Airmen's Families Association air display on 18 May 1959. A service between Leeds and Bournemouth was inaugurated in June and the airline grew by opening further services and acquiring more aircraft, but by early 1962, the airline had closed down.

The SSAFA air display at Yeadon on 18 May 1959 brought Blackburn Beverley XL148 'Y' of No.242 OCU Dishforth. The unit designation is in the diamond painted on the fin. Members of the public were allowed to walk through the interior of the Beverley to inspect its cavernous size.

Closure of the RAF Reserve Flying Schools in 1954 released a number of surplus de Havilland Chipmunks onto the civil market, especially within the UK. In 1956, G-AORF was registered; it had previously served with No.5 RFS as WB648 at Castle Bromwich near Birmingham. Bearing the operator name 'Yorkshire Flying Services Ltd', G-AORF was parked on the apron outside the municipal hangar at Yeadon on 20 August 1961. Of interest is the old style petrol pump.

B.A. Swallow G-AEVZ was built before the Second World War and used at Hedon by the Hull Aero Club. Escaping impressment by the RAF, it was stored until made airworthy at Doncaster after the war before moving to Yeadon in 1958. Usually seen in the municipal hangar, it was outside on 20 August 1961. A few years later G-AEVZ went to Crosby-on-Eden and eventually came into the hands of the Northern Aircraft Preservation Society in Stockport, which looked after it for many years. Later the aircraft was completely restored to airworthy condition and has attended a number of light aircraft rallies in southern England.

The 1962 SSAFA display at Yeadon on 11 June brought a number of fly-bys, including this Vickers Valiant B.1 XD822 from No.49 Squadron based at Marham, whose 'leaping greyhound' is shown on the fin.

Based aircraft often participated in the SSAFA displays and Miles Gemini G-AKHK was parked by the crowd barrier on 11 June 1962. In the background is the former Avro Flight Shed with a Douglas Dakota parked on the apron and the terminal building/control tower with the wartime Bellman hangars.

Ten years later, the new terminal building, apron and runway were ready. Improved facilities attracted charter flights like Aer Turas, a company based in Dublin specialising in charter flights. This Douglas C-54 Skymaster, EI-ARS, named *City of Galway*, came to Leeds Bradford in 1973, the number of service vehicles required for apron operations is aptly demonstrated. (NS)

Carriage of freight by air became a profitable activity for a number of specialised airlines and former passenger aircraft were often converted. Fred Olsen Freight, based in Norway, had this Douglas DC-6, LN-FOL which visited Leeds Bradford in 1972. (NS)

BKS Air Transport was one of the first airlines to operate from Leeds Bradford on a regular basis, they eventually became known as Northeast Airlines becoming part of the nationalised British Airways group in 1973. Services were introduced between Newcastle, Leeds Bradford and London Luton Airport. Former British European Airways Viscounts were taken into the fleet, for example, G-AOYH on the new apron in 1973. A few years later the airline lost its individual identity. (NS)

Cambrian Airways, based in Cardiff, was another regional airline which became a member of the British Airways group. Former BEA Viscounts were used on services between Leeds Bradford and Cardiff and, like Northeast Airlines, lost its separate identity in 1976. Seen in 1973 is G-AOYI with the old Avro flight shed in the background, then in use as a freight shed but demolished a few years later to make space for apron extensions. (NS)

Dan-Air of London began passenger flights between London Luton, Leeds and Glasgow in 1972 with the Avro 748. This particular aircraft, G-ARAY, was originally the second flying prototype and had been released for airline service, seen at Leeds Bradford in 1974. Dan-Air later introduced services to Cardiff. (NS)

The Civil Aviation Authority was responsible for checking out the accuracy of aeronautical navigational systems installed at airports such as at Leeds Bradford. They had a number of Hawker Siddeley 748s (as Avro had become) which could be seen regularly flying down the 'beam' on calibration work, G-AVXJ performed this duty in 1974. (NS)

SATA a Swiss carrier used this Sud Aviation Caravelle, a popular aircraft with passengers, on charter at Leeds Bradford in 1974. (NS)

The Cessna 175 Skylark was something of a rarity and G-AROC was photographed at Leeds Bradford on 28 October 1981 outside the Yorkshire Light Aircraft Ltd hangar. At this time there was a growing population of light aircraft based at the airport.

Britannia Airways was, and still is, one of the major UK charter airlines providing aircraft to the tour companies using Leeds Bradford Airport. They operated a large fleet of Boeing 737s and G-BKHF is parked on the apron extension on 11 August 1986. The earth banking is to absorb and screen aircraft noise.

An unusually quiet period enabled this photograph on 7 April 1992 of the main entrance to the Leeds Bradford Airport terminal building . The control tower is also shown.

Control Tower Sheffield 20 May 1997.

Few brand new airports have been opened in the UK since the Second World War and Sheffield has one close to the M1! It was virtually complete on 20 May 1997 and has been regularly used ever since by aircraft with a short take-off and landing capability as well as helicopters.

Seven
Civil Airfields, Gliding Sites & Museums

Civil flying in Yorkshire had become popular after the First World War, several landing strips and airfields (some having a small hangar to accommodate a few aircraft and even a club house) had been opened but upon outbreak of war all civil flying was closed down until 1946. The few aircraft which survived the war along with some ex-military aircraft were restored and the flying club movement started again – often with difficulty due to the shortage of materials and fuel. As economic conditions improved and the release of more ex-military aircraft, such as Austers, Proctors and Tiger Moths, the former airfields were re-opened. Gliding as an affordable form of flying gained in popularity.

The British aircraft industry got back into its stride building light aircraft and gliders. However, by the late 1950s/early 1960s, imports particularly from America and France added to the number of aircraft for private flying. Yorkshire was fortunate in having many discarded wartime airfields so that old runways and taxi tracks could be used whilst farmers turned the rest of the land over to agriculture. Some of these airfields have now become major centres of civil aviation, providing flying instruction as well as being used for leisure.

The 1980s also saw growth and development of aviation museums in Yorkshire, the most comprehensive being at Elvington. Nearby, Breighton houses a fine vintage aircraft collection consisting of many rare types, mostly in flying condition. Restoration light aircraft and 'warbirds'can be seen at Breighton, including aircraft undergoing maintenance. Not many visitors will realise that the airfield in the 1960s was home to Intermediate Range Ballistic Missiles and Air Defence Missiles!

Sutton Bank gliding site is one of the oldest locations where gliding activity has taken place in the UK. It has excellent facilities for the sport of flying sailplanes whether winch or air launched. Photographed on 11 June 1982.

Bagby Hangar, 11 June 1982. Bagby, near Thirsk, has been operating as a private aerodrome for more than twenty years. A brand new aerodrome created from a 'farmer's strip' has a small hangar and a caravan to serve as a club house.

Beverley (Linley Hill) was opened in August 1991 as a fully licenced airfield by the Hull Aero Club. Previous homes after the Second World War were at Speeton, Grindale and Brough. A single grass strip is provided and there are about a dozen light aircraft based at the airfield. One of the light aircraft is Cessna 172M G-BTMR with pilot Rodney Robinson in this photograph taken in September 2001. (RR)

In 1972, nearly ten years after the RAF missile units left Breighton, part of the old perimeter track was used as a runway for a crop spraying aircraft. Piper Pawnee G- AZIE was based for a few years, seen above on 19 September 1972.

Opened by Hornet Aviation in about 1980, The Real Aeroplane Co. Ltd has developed a light aircraft centre at Breighton about the area of the former crop-spraying business. Excellent hangarage and engineering facilities have been created as well as a grass runway and spectator facilities.

The collection of aircraft under the care of The Real Aeroplane Co. Ltd at Breighton includes several rare types which have been imported. The Nanchang CJ-6A was imported from China and carries an appropriate colour scheme as '2028'. It was actually registered in the UK as G-BVVF, 13 September 1999.

Spitfire PR.XI PL965 being overhauled on 3 September 2001 at Breighton. This aircraft is painted in a pink colour scheme and is one of the rare earlier photographic versions of the Spitfire. Bought by the Royal Netherlands Air Force after the Second World War, it was later restored by an RAF team in Germany before going back to the Dutch museum. The next stage in its life was acquisition in Britain and restored to flying condition, being civilian registered as G-MKXI and painted in the PR scheme.

The Aeronca 100 G-AEVS, a pre-war light aircraft, has had several homes and now resides at Breighton. Photographed on 27 February 1994.

Breighton, 27 February 1994. Quite a large number of the American 1940s/1950s built Luscombe Silvaires have been imported into the UK during the last twenty years. Many owners have been able to obtain unused 'period' registrations as shown on G-AKVP rather than have modern or personalised registration.

Elvington began as a temporary RAF airfield. No.77 (Bomber) Squadron with Halifaxes was there for eighteen months before the base was handed over to two French squadrons serving with the RAF. It was retained after the Second World War for a variety of purposes, including rebuilding as a USAF base and as a RLG for local RAF flying schools. Taken over by the Yorkshire Air Museum, this has ensured its continued existence for aviation purposes. The control tower (drawing 4532/43) has been totally renovated and restored with similar wartime equipment. Photographed on 13 August 1986.

The airfield site at Elvington was totally rebuilt in 1954 for the United States Air Force with a new runway, massive aircraft parking area and a new control tower mounted on stilts. It was not used operationally except by RAF aircraft as a RLG for 'touch and go's'. (AB)

One of the major projects undertaken at the Yorkshire Air Museum at Elvington has been the construction of the Handley Page Halifax static replica, painted up to commemorate an aircraft flown by No.158 (Bomber) Squadron which was based at Yorkshire airfields from 1942 to 1945. Serialled LV907 and coded NP-F, the aircraft is named *Friday The Thirteenth* and seen here on 17 August 1995 in the small workshop. The complete aircraft now takes pride of place in the 'new' T2 hangar which was erected at Elvington in 1996.

The French Air Force donated this Dassault Mirage III as a reminder of the French connection with Elvington., serialled No.538 and coded 3-QH, 24 April 1996. The 'new' T2 hangar brought from Kemble is being clad enabling many of the aircraft previously kept in the open to be brought under cover.

Flown into Elvington for the Yorkshire Air Museum on 25 November 1993 was Handley Page Victor K.2 XL231 *Lusty Linda* which had served with a number of bomber squadrons prior to conversion to a flying tanker. In the later role, XL231 was involved in the Falklands War in 1982 and the Gulf War in 1991. Photographed on 17 August 1997.

Tribute to the Buccaneer and its service history especially in the Gulf War is made by XX901, displayed in a pink colour scheme and carrying the markings 'Kathryn-The Flying Mermaid'. The new Elvington hangar is an excellent exhibition hall as seen here on 11 April 1999.

Full Sutton opened in May 1944 when No.77 (Bomber) Squadron moved over from Elvington. The airfield was retained by the RAF and used as an Advanced Flying School with Gloster Meteors in the 1950s before it was taken over by RAF Driffield as Thor missile base. The control tower (drawing 343/43), derelict on 19 September 1972, still retained the old runway 'in use' boards from the RAF flying school days. It has been totally renovated and now used for commercial purposes.

Part of the taxiway and grass area at Full Sutton was taken over as a private airfield in the 1990s and now houses several light aircraft, flying mainly at weekends.

Situated on the moors above Bridlington is Grindale airfield, used mainly for the leisure pursuit of parachuting and some microlight flying. Cessna 206 Super Skywagon G-ASVN, an aircraft originally developed for carrying a number of passengers and/or light freight, is ideal for parachuting; photographed on 12 June 1981.

The population of light aircraft at Crossland Moor included this French-built Jodel DR.100A Ambassadeur touring aircraft G-BFBA on 29 October 1987.

Netherthorpe was licenced as a civil aerodrome in 1935, its wartime history was brief and the site abandoned until it was re-opened in the 1960s as a civil airfield by the Netherthorpe Aero Club (then the Sheffield Aero Club). It was a thriving centre for light aircraft and a flying school, as well as an excellent club house. The pre-war hangars survive and are used for aircraft maintenance, seen above on 9 March 1993.

This Cessna 150 G-AWAW at Netherthorpe in August 1981 was in for some maintenance work; it was usually based at Felixkirk near Thirsk. It was one of the first aircraft built at the Rheims (France) factory which produced a large number of Cessna types in the last thirty years and, in 1990 ,G-AWAW was selected for static display in the Flight Laboratory Gallery in the London South Kensington Museum. To the rear are the original pre-war hangars.

The Clutton FRED (Flying Runabout Experimental Design) is a home-built aircraft to a design by Eric Clutton; construction of G-USTY was started in Birmingham. It was based at Netherthorpe, being painted in pseudo-RAF military markings, 16 April 1981.

Based at Netherthorpe in 1986 for a short period was this Dornier Do 28 executive twin-engined transport.

The Sheffield Aero Club, based at Netherthorpe, uses a variety of aircraft for flying instruction including this Cessna 152 G-BRNK, 1 May 1995.

Aeronca Champion G-BTNO based at Netherthorpe still carries as a souvenir its American registration N84441, 9 March 1993.

A scaled down replica of the famous Mustang fighter, the fuselage of the home-built Bonsall Mustang appeared at Netherthorpe in about 1986 and work slowly progressed, with the aircraft being completed in the early 1990s. A fictitious code and serial are applied in lieu of its civil registration, G-BDWM, which had been allocated as long ago as 1976.

Many Chipmunks found their way to civilian owners over the years when the RAF disposed of them. G-BBWN was painted up in RAF markings; it seems the serial WZ876 is not shown quite correctly. Photographed on 1 May 1995 at Netherthorpe, the aircraft was unfortunately damaged in a landing at nearby Thorpe Salvin early the following year and the aircraft was later dismantled for spares use.

Imported from America and flying as N870MC this home-built Steen Skybolt gained a British registration of G-BRIS in 1989 and was based at Netherthorpe on 9 March 1993.

Visiting the maintenance company at Netherthorpe on 20 May 1997 was this Auster 6A G-ARIH/TW591, normally resident on a private air-strip in Staffordshire. It wears the markings of an Auster AOP.6 (despite the silver markings with a yellow training band) of No.664 (AOP) Squadron of the Royal Auxiliary Air Force, which had detached flights at Yeadon and Rufforth. Just behind the Auster is a Polish-built Wilga G-BXBZ in for maintenance.

Building of Pocklington RAF aerodrome started in 1939 as a permanent station. It was occupied by various bomber squadrons in No.4 (B) Group until it was closed down in 1946. The original control tower was removed as it was too close to the new runways and this building (343/43) was erected across the airfield. It became derelict quite quickly when the airfield was closed. Photographed on 6 August 1980, it is now demolished.

This imposing memorial is located in the area taken over by the Wolds Gliding Club which uses a large part of the airfield at Pocklington. It commemorates the connection of No.102 (Ceylon) (Bomber) Squadron RAF and No.405 (Vancouver) Squadron RCAF with Pocklington. No.405 opened the aerodrome in 1941, with Wellingtons, before being replaced by No.102, which flew Halifaxes from 1942 to 1945.

Scheibe Falke G-BGMV, photographed on 4 June 1979, had just been received by the Wolds Gliding Club. In developing this part of Pocklington airfield, the Club erected a hangar and later more accommodation with a caravan site for glider pilots.

The Wolds Gliding Club obtained this Slingsby Venture G-OWGC, with a personalised registration as an ex-RAF aircraft in 1991. The former permanent RAF J Type hangar remains along with some of the temporary T2 hangars, all in use for industrial purposes, they had been retained after the war for storage purposes.

Rufforth was a Second World War airfield opened in 1943 for No.4 (B) Group. After operations by No.158 (Bomber) Squadron for a few months, it became the base of a training unit converting crews to the Halifax under Marston Moor base. Retained after the war, it has been used for a variety of purposes by the RAF, such as administration, storage of equipment and a RLG for both Linton-on-Ouse and Church Fenton. Use of Rufforth for gliding operations was permitted by the RAF and this Slingsby T.21 Glider of the Ouse Gliding Club was present on 27 June 1970. The VCR had not yet been mounted on the control tower. (NS)

The control tower (drawing 13079/41) was modified by the addition of a VCR during the later RAF operations and again modified for filming the *Airline* TV series by applying camouflage. In more recent years the original airfield site has been divided between microlight flying and glider operations.

Cyclone Pegasus G-OHKS microlight aircraft, 6 September 2001, in the area of Rufforth airfield used for operations of this type of aircraft.

Moving out along the strip taxiway to the runway at Rufforth on 6 September 2001 was this two seat Scheibe Falke G-BODU. The pilot is Brian Pritchard, an instructor on this type of aircraft which is owned by the Monica English Trust and operated in association with the York Gliding Centre.

Aircraft maintenance facilities at Rufforth are provided by McLean Aviation which has its own hangar and site but uses the 'glider' airfield. The aircraft is a Socata Rallye Club G-BIOR, 6 September 2001.

Gliders, once the wings are detached, can be stored in a very small space. Three aircraft are seen here in the McLean Aviation hangar at Rufforth on 6 September 2001.

The Croydon-based firm of Rollason began building the French Druine Condor and many of these were rented out to flying clubs, G-AWEI was seen at Sherburn on 21 September 1972. Another French design, the Jodel was seen at Sherburn; one is also parked on the grass in front of the former ATA hangar.

Being refuelled on 11 September 1973 at Sherburn is this Cessna 150 Commuter G-BAEU, built in France. By this time Sherburn boasted several Cessna aircraft.

American-built aircraft, such as the AA.5 Traveler G-BCEO, were imported in crates and re-assembled. Several of these aircraft were to be seen around Sherburn, 16 July 1975. Behind are the buildings of Lennerton Farm, partly used by the Air Transport Auxiliary during the Second World War.

Tiger Moth G-ANON was one of the large batch to be released from the RAF in 1954 when the RAF Reserve Schools were disbanded. Civilianised it eventually found its way to Sherburn and restored into these military markings as T-7909 and has been used in film work, as well as attending air displays. In June 1999 T-7909 (with crew!) flew from Yorkshire to Prague. The round trip took twenty hours flying time, apparently this was the second time she had made such a journey.

The Sherburn Aero Club has used several standard training types from the Condor to various models of the Cessna and a fleet of Piper Cadets with a 'personalised' series of registrations, G-SACS. Photographed on 7 April 1992.

Becoming a rarity is the Auster breed compared with the large numbers seen in the 1950s. Autocrat G-AJRC was usually kept in the new hangar by the old Eastern Aviation hangar at Sherburn, seen above on 25 April 1994.

Helicopter training has been undertaken at Sherburn since the early 1970s and is done now on a regular basis. The Robinson R.22 Beta G-HIEL, a popular aircraft, is seen above on 25 April 1994.

Sherburn has developed into a major light aircraft centre providing a multitude of facilities, from pilot training to maintenance and housing of aircraft. A well-appointed club house caters for members and welcomes the aviation minded public as well.

Eight
Aircraft Manufacturers' Airfields

Blackburn Aircraft Ltd

The principal aircraft manufacturing company in Yorkshire became Blackburn Aircraft Ltd after the First World War, with premises in Leeds and at Brough. During the Second World War the company managed the shadow aircraft factory at Sherburn-in-Elmet, building approximately 1,700 Fairey Swordfish. At Brough more than 600 Fairey Barracudas were built in addition to their own design of the Botha, a Repair & Modification Organisation was also operated. Production of the Blackburn Firebrand torpedo fighter continued up to 1947.

Blackburn then amalgamated with General Aircraft Ltd of Feltham, bringing with it the Universal Freighter and subsequent production of the Beverley (forty-seven built) at Brough. Contracts were received for aircraft components to assist other manufacturers and, in addition, between 1948 and 1958 the company at Brough built 125 Percival Prentice and 30 Boulton Paul Balliol training aircraft for the RAF.

The most successful aircraft designed and built post-war by the company has been the NA.39 or Buccaneer for the Royal Navy and RAF; a number were sold abroad. Construction commenced in 1956 and Holme-on-Spalding Moor airfield was taken over as a test base. Blackburn came under the Hawker Siddeley banner in 1963 and was responsible for the in-service support and modification of the McDonnell Phantom procured in 1967 for the Royal Navy and the RAF. Holme-on-Spalding Moor was vacated by the company in 1983. In more recent years, Brough, through British Aerospace and now BAE Systems, has made a considerable contribution to the manufacture of aircraft such as the Harrier and Hawk as well as updating work on these types.

A.V. Roe & Co. Ltd

Yeadon, the airport opened by the Leeds and Bradford Corporations, was taken over by A.V. Roe & Co. Ltd in the Second World War to manage the huge shadow aircraft factory for the production of the Avro Anson. The first aircraft was completed in the middle of 1941. Concurrent with Anson production, Avro Lancasters, Avro Yorks and a few Avro Lincolns were built during the war years. Afterwards the Avro XIX, a civil version of the Anson, was built and Avro Yorks were produced for civil customers. Nearly 5,000 aircraft were built in the Yeadon factory, and it was announced in April 1946 that the factory was to close by the end of the year with the loss of about 5,000 jobs. The semi-sunk factory still exists and has been used by a number of industrial firms; the final assembly hangars and flight sheds were demolished in the 1960s to make way for airport developments.

Slingsby Sailplanes Ltd

Formed prior to the Second World War, Slingsby Sailplanes Ltd of Kirbymoorside is one of the foremost UK companies producing gliders and sailplanes. Through a variety of owners they became Slingsby Aviation Ltd and built a series of powered aircraft from motorised gliders to the T.67 Firefly, used for training by both military and civilian operators. Kirbymoorside has also seen work done on light aircraft and replicas for film use.

Torva Sailplanes Ltd was formed in 1969 to build sailplanes of then a special type of construction. The first prototype was flown at RAF Driffield on 8 May 1971 and a number of aircraft were built, one reported to be in store at Rufforth airfield. Unfortunately, the company closed down shortly afterwards. A new company, Europa Aviation, has a range of light aircraft supplied as kits, particularly to the overseas market. Flying is carried out at Kirbymoorside.

The original factory buildings at Brough, enlarged during the Second World War are ranged along the shore of the Humber estuary. A disused flying boat slipway still exists. The flying school hangars are identified centre bottom (the view is approximately from the north-east) with the asphalt runway running between the two parts of the complex. A grass runway 06/24 is available adjacent to the massive car park. (Brough Heritage Centre)

The Universal Freighter had its first flight at Brough on 20 June 1950. Capacity to carry large loads is demonstrated by the coach on the integral ramp at Brough. The type was ordered by the RAF as the Beverley. (BRR/Brough Heritage Centre)

Design of the Blackburn B-2 originated by developing the Bluebird light aircraft into a side-by-side seat trainer in 1931. More than forty aircraft were built, many serving with the Blackburn flying schools at Brough and Hanworth. Only a few survived the war, including G-AEBJ which has been kept in superb condition and has attended many air-shows to the delight of the watching public. (Brough Heritage Centre)

This view taken in 1997 of the flying school building at Brough also shows the row of hangars fronting the airfield which were used originally to house the flying school. The airfield control room surmounts the building which is typical 1930s design and construction. (BD)

Left: Brough is still an active airfield and surrounded by public paths. This sign is located on the north side of the airfield overlooking the asphalt runway 12/30.

Royal Navy Historic Flight, Fairey Swordfish II W5856 (G-BMGC) coded 'A2A' and painted to represent an aircraft of No.810 Squadron prior to the Second World War. This particular aircraft (although it did not serve with No.810 Squadron Fleet Air Arm) is a Blackburn-built example and was eventually shipped to Canada, placed in store then sold after the war for civil use. It was bought in 1977 by the Strathallan Collection, returned to the UK for restoration, obtained by the Royal Navy Historic Flight and passed to Brough in 1991 for complete restoration to flying condition. Brough finished the job in May 1993 and handed the aircraft over to join the other famous Swordfish LS326, also Blackburn-built. (Brough Heritage Centre)

The Sea Fury VR930 of the Royal Navy Historic Flight, based at Yeovilton was brought to Brough for restoration to flying standard which was achieved in 1998. It is painted in the colour scheme appropriate to the Korean war, No.802 Squadron, Fleet Air Arm operating from HMS Ocean on behalf of the United Nations. (Brough Heritage Centre)

Holme-on-Spalding Moor airfield, wartime home of RAF bomber squadrons, was taken over by Blackburn in 1957 for development work including test-flying production Buccaneers. Ordered originally for the Royal Navy, the RAF also ordered a land version, later taking over the naval aircraft. No.12 Squadron RAF began operating Buccaneers in October 1969 from Honington in Suffolk, mainly in the maritime attack role, it transferred to Lossiemouth in Scotland. The type lasted until the early 1990s when the entire fleet was taken out of service and many 'reduced to produce'. (Brough Heritage Centre)

At Holme-on-Spalding Moor, nearest aircraft is the SEPECAT Jaguar-built in the UK by British Aircraft Corporation at Warton in Lancashire. This aircraft coded '18' was used by the RAF Operational Conversion Unit. Behind is a McDonnell Phantom, a Royal Navy development aircraft. Hawker Siddeley Brough was nominated as the 'aircraft weapons system sister firm' when the Royal Navy/RAF Phantom fleet was bought from America, with deliveries starting in 1967. (Brough Heritage Centre)

Avro Jig & Tool Drawing Office Staff in front of York, November 1945. From left to right, back: Messrs Niad, Jarvis, Farrar, Poole, Green, Barker, Chomley, Hird, J.Marshall, Asquith, Grange, Richardson, Doreen Eagan, Kell, Metcalf, Durkells, Crowther, Berrington, Lamb, Woodford, Whitely, Barrass, Parker, Stableford, Cocking, Hart, Holmes, Burnett, Donaldson, Rymes. Front: Chief Draughtsman, R.P. Dodsworth. (J.H. Kell via GM)

Avro Nineteens G-AGZT and G-AGUD in the A.V. Roe & Co. Ltd Flight Shed at Yeadon being prepared for flight testing and delivery. (R. Marshall via GM)

Right: Yeadon control tower and terminal building with the Avro Flight Sheds hidden from view. The small building on top of the hangar is the wartime firewatcher's office, camouflage still clear in Summer 1946. (R. Scratchard via GM)

'Slingsby', through various owners has been at Kirbymoorside. The factory has grown and produced not only a range of sailplanes but powered aircraft, from flying film replicas to the Firefly which is in current production. (MJR)

Export Slingsby Firefly was flown in test marks as G-7-114 before coming HB-NBD. Unfortunately the aircraft was written off on 12 September 1987. (MJR)

Nine
Lost & Forgotten Airfields

Acaster Malbis aerodrome, close to York, was used mainly as a bomber training airfield developed from a small grass airfield at the beginning of the Second World War. Closed down in 1945, its runways and buildings were used to store explosives until disposed. In the 1980s, part of a runway was used by private aircraft, particularly on race days at York. A visible reminder is the control tower (Air Ministry drawing 343/43) here in May 1970.

Carnaby was built as a wartime emergency airfield with a huge runway to accept damaged aircraft returning from operations in the Second World War. Retained after the war, it was used extensively by RAF Driffield. A flying club was established in the 1950s but Carnaby was required by the RAF to station Thor and Bloodhound missiles from 1959 to 1963. Afterwards, the whole of the runway was developed as an industrial area with little remaining.

Catfoss was opened in 1932 and, throughout its life, used for operational training particularly in connection with armaments. During a major rebuilding operation in 1941/42, a new control tower (Air Ministry drawing 12779/41) was erected which still survives although to some extent derelict. Closed at the end of the war, the RAF took over again for use as a Thor missile base from 1959 to 1963. Photographed in 1998.

Many of the wartime buildings at Catfoss still exist, including the pre-war and war time hangars which have been converted for industrial purposes. Some of the smaller buildings, only intended for wartime service, have been renovated for commercial use. The Parachute Store building looking good in 2001. (RR)

Cottam was not used operationally despite being built as a No.4 (B) Group airfield. The control tower (Air Ministry drawing 13726/41), being the only reminder in post-war years, is now demolished and forgotten. Photographed on 12 September 1973.

During the First World War, an aerodrome existed at Doncaster Racecourse; it had wooden bowstrung truss hangars, one of which later survived opposite the racecourse. In the 1970s it was used as a bus garage. Photographed on 5 September 1976, it is now demolished.

Dalton was a satellite of Topcliffe for operations, but was transferred to the RCAF to convert bomber crews to operational types. Closing at the end of the war, industrial use was made of the hangars, especially this B.2 which had been erected for major maintenance and repair work; it was used for storage on 5 June 1980. A similar hangar has recently been totally renovated at Catfoss.

A new municipal airport for Doncaster was opened in 1934 next to the football ground, it was served by both internal and an international air service. After the Second World War, operations were mainly by private aircraft although the original terminal and control tower was used for a while. Photographed on 4 May 1978, it was demolished a few years later; most the whole of the aerodrome site is covered by new building developments.

Doncaster Airport had a number of flying clubs, Cessna 150s and a Grumman AA.5 on 16 June 1981 outside one of the massive concrete hangars constructed before the Second World War. The Doncaster Aero Club which controlled the airfield had to vacate these hangars due to the first redevelopment of the site.

New hangars and a club house were erected on the opposite side of Doncaster Airport, a large number of light aircraft were based in addition to flying club aircraft. Auster J/1N G-AJIU wears pseudo military marks on 16 April 1991. The aerodrome was finally closed at the end of 1992.

East Moor was an operational No.4 Group bomber station transferring to the Canadians. After the end of the war it was taken over by the RAF for No.54 OTU which later transferred to RAF Leeming. By the end of 1946, the airfield had been abandoned and the technical areas became overgrown. The control tower (drawing 13079/41) was derelict when photographed 1997; it is now demolished. (BD)

Holme-on-Spalding Moor opened in 1940 had a degree of permanent buildings such as the 'J' Type hangar. After the operational squadrons left, it was used for explosives storage for a period, then for flying training and ultimately as the test and development airfield of Hawker Siddeley Aviation Ltd at Brough. The memorial situated in the old technical area, now being used by commercial and industrial companies, records No.76 (Bomber) Squadron whose base it was for two years.

Paull aerodrome near Hull existed for several years and was used by Hull Aero Club, but it is now closed. The first production Beverley C.1, XB259 never served with the RAF but was used for development flying and civil charter work. It was moved to Paull for preservation where it was photographed on 12 April 1977. Now preserved and moved to the Museum of Army Transport in Flemingate, Beverley, East Yorkshire, it is the only Beverley to survive. (NS)

Hutton Cranswick was built as a fighter station to replace Leconfield which had temporarily transferred to Fighter Command in the early part of the Second World War. Abandoned in 1946, the control tower (drawing 12779/41) eventually was converted to a house but is still recognisable. (BD)

Bomber operations started at Lissett in 1943 and continued to the end of the war, abandoned like so many others and used for explosive storage until these were all disposed. A few buildings still remain but a memorial to No.158 (Bomber) Squadron which operated at Lissett 1943/45 is in the adjacent church yard.

Marston Moor was opened in 1941 with the control tower (drawing 518/40) is still fully recognisable. The airfield site is extensively used as a Motor Sport Training School. Never used by operational squadrons but for conversion of crews to operational aircraft, the tradition of training continues! Many dispersed buildings along with the hangars survive and full use being made for industrial purposes.

Derelict for many years the Melbourne Control Tower (drawing FCW 4514) is slowly being restored, possibly as a small museum. Part of the airfield has been used by a light aircraft as strip but most of it has returned to agriculture. (BD)

No.10 (Bomber) Squadron RAF made its base at Melbourne from 1942 to 1945 and its association is commemorated by this fitting memorial placed by the main entrance to the airfield.

Not a lot is left at Riccall! Opened as a No.4 (B) Group temporary training station, it was quickly abandoned at the end of the Second World War. Part converted to a recreational area, most of the buildings have gone but this solitary hut, which was photographed in the mid-1990s.

Snaith, opened in 1940, has few remaining buildings except the hangars, two T2 types (as shown above, 30 May 1979) and a 'J' Type. Prime use after the Second World War was as a Home Office Storage Depot. A memorial is located in the grounds of Selby Abbey.

Skipton-on-Swale Control Tower (drawing 12096/41) looks over the former airfield which was used exclusively by Canadian squadrons in Bomber Command from 1942. It closed in 1945 and abandoned. (BD)

Other than a brief presence of a flight from an RAF squadron in 1940, Tholthorpe was a Canadian base until the end of the war. Above is the original watch office (drawing 13079/41) with large 'runway in use' marker boards, it was replaced by a larger control tower when the station was re-built. Both buildings still exist.

Thornaby-on-Tees opened in the late 1920s as a flying training school. No.608 (North Riding) Squadron Auxiliary Air Force formed there in 1937 and, throughout the war, was used by Coastal Command squadrons. No.608 (North Riding) Squadron reformed afterwards with Mosquitoes, Spitfires, then Vampire jet fighters until disbandment of the Royal Auxiliary Air Force in 1957. Also used by No.205 AFS at Middleton St George as a RLG, the last service unit (No.92 Squadron with Hawker Hunters) left towards the end of 1958 and the airfield closed down to be completely developed for housing and industrial purposes. Many of the buildings still remain, such as hangars and those like the Station Headquarters, which dates from the opening of the aerodrome. (DBF)

The York municipal Airport opened in 1936 and a small hangar with technical buildings was erected, requisitioned and used by the RAF; its main use during the Second World War was as a massive Handley Page Halifax bomber repair unit. A little flying took place after the war until closed in 1955. This hangar did survive as a farmer's store but demolished when the whole aerodrome site was developed in the 1980s for housing, and later industrial and commercial premises, a process which is virtually complete. Some of the wartime factory hangars exist in use.